EUROPE'S FUTURE:
The Grand Alternatives

DAVID P. CALLEO

The Norton Library   NEW YORK

W · W · NORTON & COMPANY · INC ·

BOOKS THAT LIVE

The Norton imprint on a book means that in the publisher's
estimation it is a book not for a single season but for the years.

W. W. NORTON & COMPANY, INC.

SBN 393 00406 6

Printed in the United States of America
3 4 5 6 7 8 9 0

Dav ... w York.
He ... iversity
in 1 ... fellow-
ship ... cil and
the ... *leridge*
and ... *tlantic*
Fan

To my Father and Mother

Contents

Europe's Future examines the "grand alternatives" proposed for European unity and relates them to persisting political and intellectual traditions. It is thus an historical study of postwar politics and political thought. But it was also written with a further purpose in mind. None of the major alternative ideals for the future seems an adequate guide for the colossal task of forging political union in Western Europe. Atlanticists, Eurocrats, and Gaullists all present too partial a view of modern Western history and politics. Yet the nationalist and federalist ideals each have much that is relevant, wise, and noble. Any inspired policy for Europe must build upon the insights of them all. A dispassionate study of the conflicting ideals would, it was hoped, contribute to more informed views in America and Britain about Europe's quest for unity, and possibly more constructive policies for coming to terms with it.

Now, a year after the book was originally published, it is difficult to say either that the fundamental issues or schools of thought are greatly changed or that the need for imaginative new policies is any less. With Britain again seeking to enter the Common Market, it seems all the more urgent to transcend the old misunderstandings. But relations among the major Western powers seem today, more than ever, a conversation among deaf men — a depressing dialogue full of misunderstanding and incomprehension.

If the past year has not changed the alternatives for union, has it altered the prospects? To many observers, the present trend of events is not, on balance, encouraging. Unfavorable signs are certainly not difficult to find. The steady erosion of the Atlantic

Alliance, the disunity of the Six, and the persistent political malaise in so many European countries are all discouraging enough. Even the good news has its dark side. In spite of its apparent conversion to the Common Market, Britain's Labour Government still appears to many a most diffident partisan of European political integration. And the great Gaullist drive to open up Eastern Europe, however desirable in itself, could greatly complicate the task of Western unity.

All in all, it is tempting to believe that the cynics have been right all along: Stalin was Europe's real federator; now that the spur of terror is gone, so is the thrust toward unity. Failure is not, after all, an unusual fate for grand designs. Events generally overtake plans. But nations do occasionally direct rather than endure history. In any event, the actions of this generation will probably determine Europe's place in the world for a long time to come. For both sides of the Atlantic, the problem of Europe's fate remains a splendid challenge and a most awesome responsibility.

Nuffield College, Oxford   David P. Calleo
November, 1966

This is a book written not to predict Europe's future, but to explain the major ways of looking at it. Among other things, I have sought to be an historian of ideas, hoping to seek out sympathetically the broad views that lie behind policies and statements. One of the few advantages for the historian of the present is being able to talk directly to those who create the ideals or manage the power. I owe much to several politicians, writers, and civil servants who kindly made themselves available for one or more long and generous talks. Obviously, they are not responsible for any of my conclusions, and, in several cases, they would disagree with most of them. I should like to thank Raymond Aron, General Pierre Billotte, Henri Brugmans, Alastair Buchan, Donald Cook, Dunstan Curtis, Sir Alec Douglas-Home, Bertrand de Jouvenel, Albert Kervyn de Lettenhove, J. M. A. H. Luns, Richard Mayne, Pierre Mendès-France, Roger Nathan, Roy Pryce, Robert Salmon, Altiero Spinelli, Michael Stewart, and Jean Touchard.

Some of the most useful interviews of all have been with a number of extremely able officials at the Common Market Commission, the Quai d'Orsay, the British Foreign Office and the Dutch Foreign Ministry. As civil servants, they would doubtless prefer their kindness to rest unacknowledged. I am grateful, as well, for talks with officials of the State Department stationed in Europe.

I must thank Professors Karl W. Deutsch, Jean Touchard and Nicholas Wahl for useful suggestions at critical stages, and Heinz Koeppler, not only for his advice but for his invitation to an admirable seminar in Wilton Park which started me on this book.

Acknowledgments

I am grateful to my friends and colleagues who have been helpful in suggesting and arranging interviews, in particular to Simon Bowes Lyon, Ralph G. E. Jarvis, and Professor Eugene V. Rostow.

The project was financed chiefly by the Rockefeller Foundation, with generous help from Yale University's Stimson Fund. My work in Paris was greatly assisted by the kind hospitality of the Centre Universitaire International.

Finally, I gratefully acknowledge the helpful suggestions, long hours and careful work of my research assistant, Douglas Crowley. As for my long-suffering friends, upon whom my conversation constantly forces the burden of my thoughts, I console myself with the hope that de Gaulle has been less of a bore than Coleridge.

July 26, 1965   *D.P.C.*
Lluch Alcari

I.

Europe's Future, the Battle of Ideals

I.

Europe's Future,
the Battle
of Ideals

Scarcely a generation ago, it was fashionable to write books about the death of Europe. Its history in the twentieth century was a sad chronicle of instability and self-mutilation. The lights that had gone out in 1914 never did burn brightly after Versailles. The Second World War left the old continent in physical and spiritual ruin. It was easy to believe, as Roosevelt apparently did, that in the postwar world Europe would not count for much.

Doubtless American generosity was crucial. Nevertheless, Europe's rapid economic recovery in both East and West was a great surprise. Indeed, by 1950, a detached observer might have found Europe one of the few bright spots in a world panorama that was otherwise extremely somber. The thoughtful observer, looking back on the whole half century, might well have concluded that not since the seventeenth century had politics and warfare so completely escaped from rational human control. Man's growing ability to dominate nature had only exacerbated the consequences of his lack of control over himself. Science's contribution to politics had made tyranny more effective and wars increasingly destructive. In 1950, the chances seemed feeble for a lasting international stability that could avoid war. Communism continued to be as virulently aggressive as ever. And while the underdeveloped world was in a ferment of "rising expectations," the gap between rich and poor countries was increasing and any hope for progress seemed ruled out by the apparently uncontrollable growth of population. In short, man seemed less able than ever to gain rational control over the social and political forces which, if unchecked, would bring about his ruin.

But Europe in 1950 was already well on its way to economic recovery and, most encouraging of all, there seemed genuine prospects for its peaceful political union. Public opinion in Europe strongly supported some form of unity and European enthusiasts occupied innumerable critical positions in political and economic life. Indeed, the two great Allied leaders, Churchill and de Gaulle, and the two new leaders of the defeated, Adenauer and de Gasperi, were all proponents of some form of European union. There had just been established in 1949 what some hoped was the nascent federal government, the Council of Europe.

In the ensuing years the European movement has had many successes. While direct attempts at political or military integration have made little headway, the creation of the Coal and Steel Community in 1950 opened the promising vista of political unity through economic integration. The dream of so many centuries, a single European community, would it seemed finally be realized, not through brutal conquest by the strongest, but by the gentler logic of economic forces. The idea behind the Coal and Steel Community progressed further with the Common Market in 1958. The rapid success of these institutions was striking. With the European economy booming, the schedule of economic integration was speeded up. A great spate of engagingly optimistic books appeared, spouting alphabetical agencies and smiling statistics, and predicting the imminent unification of Europe through the magic of the celebrated "spill-over effect." It would be impossible to reverse the economic integration, it was argued, since the cost to any one of the partners would be too great. Furthermore, the economic meshing would inevitably demand unified political policies and hence the political institutions to reach them. Political union was therefore imminent.

The high point of optimism came when Great Britain, which had steadily opposed, hindered, or ignored most of these European arrangements, reversed itself and applied for admission to the Common Market. But the moment of triumph was the beginning of discord. De Gaulle's brutal veto of Britain's entry in early 1963 angered and frightened his partners, and his alliance with Adenauer conjured up the image of a Europe dominated by France and Germany. A split developed over the plans for political union and the Dutch torpedoed the Fouchet Plan. The Americans began talking more and more about Atlantic unity and less and less about European.

Since de Gaulle's veto and the failure of the Fouchet Plan, no progress whatever has been made towards political unity. Indeed, the prospects have steadily been growing worse. Nationalism is once again stirring in Europe. After fifteen years of practical achievement, the European movement is moribund. Why? No one openly favors a return to the old Europe of nationalist assertion, competition, and conflict. Reason continues to dictate some form of unity as probably the only way to avoid internal wars and external domination. If Europe does fragment into its nationalist pieces, it will be in spite of the professed sentiments of nearly all of Europe's political leaders, including the chief "nationalist," General de Gaulle—himself an author of a recent plan for European unity.

It is common practice to blame the present impasse in Europe on de Gaulle's obstinately aboriginal nationalism. But the questions he has raised are not without substance. What are the limits of a workable community? To what extent can it be merged into "Atlantic partnership" without losing any meaningful cohesion?

What is the difference between a free-trade area and a community? Can the democratic authority, the legitimacy of national governments, be transferred to a supranational creation? What sort of policies would be likely to result from such a government? Would or should it be independent of American control?

If nothing else, de Gaulle has raised the issues that have always been waiting in the ambiguous and conflicting terms, programs, and motives of the whole postwar movement. He has, in fact, forced the partisans of unity to contemplate the fundamental questions. What is a political community? What does it need to be effective? What role will a European community play in the world?

Although nearly everyone in Europe has come out for it and there were few in the United States who did not regard it almost as an end in itself, the ideal of European unity has all along meant quite different things to different people. The moment for making significant choices, for choosing one path and not another, apparently draws nearer. That is, perhaps, in itself a great tribute to the effectiveness of the Communities. At such a time, it is not surprising that discussions become more intense and the participants more embittered. The heritage of facile but ambiguous terms and slogans dogs the effort to find the right way out. If the academic has any place in the world of contemporary politics, it is to clarify the alternatives. It should be left to the politician to create consensus by confusion.

This book is a study of the major approaches to building the new political community. It is a study of the "grand alternatives" now being proposed to the Europeans—the Atlantic Europe of NATO (North Atlantic Treaty Organization) and MLF (Multilateral Nuclear Force), the supranational Europe of the Common Market, or the Europe of States of General de Gaulle. Each of these grand alternatives proposes for Europe a new form of political community beyond the nation and each sets forth a method for building it. Behind the goal and the method lie fundamental assumptions about what constitutes a desirable modern political community, and implied in each approach is a view of Europe's place in the world of the future.

Each of the grand alternatives suffers, I believe, from a distinctive weakness. Each in its own way is an imperfect ideal and therefore an inadequate guide to the future. The bitter conflict between these ideals is standing in the way of any further progress towards unity. The ideal of some form of organized European community is, of course, extremely complex. Doubtless, no ideal is ever adequate. Life always eludes man's tidy abstractions and many good things have been built by practical men following bad theories. Nevertheless, the role of theory is to guide practice, to be the weapon by which man gains control over his own affairs and directs his efforts towards goals he understands. With ideals, man can become the master rather than the slave of history. Europe today, like Hamilton's America, is about "to decide the important question, whether societies of men are really capable or not of establishing good government from reflection and choice, or whether they are forever destined to depend for their political constitutions on accident and force." [1]

But politics remains always the art of the possible. Ideals are good not only because they correspond to abstract universal notions about what is desirable, but because they are fashioned to call up from an actual society the best that is in it. Utopian ideals that ignore what is possible are useless in giving man rational control over his own environment. That was the great wisdom of Tocqueville, who, while not altogether pleased by the advent of democracy, bent his efforts to guiding it towards an ideal form which would elicit its advantages and minimize its defects.

It is in this spirit that I have undertaken this study of the grand alternatives. I make no pretense at answering the great questions, but I do plan to raise them and to suggest their significance. Such a study will, I hope, be a useful contribution to that reflection which must precede rational and purposeful choice.

II.

Nationalism vs. Federalism in Postwar Europe

II.

Nationalism
vs. Federalism
in Postwar Europe

The unification of Europe may be a daring program, but it is scarcely a new idea. It has been a recurrent dream since the Middle Ages, inspiring would-be conquerors, well-meaning philosophers, and occasional visionary statesmen.[1] But no one has yet been able to force or persuade the European to unite beyond the framework of the national state. It has been possible to unify France, Germany, and Italy, but not Europe, and not even Austria-Hungary. The organizing principle of modern Europe has not been the unity of federalism, but the independence of nationalism.

1.

Few modern political theorists praise nationalism. Writers who denounce nationalism indiscriminately often seem to overlook the fact that by any reasonable definition, the great majority of people in the United States or Britain are nationalists—which is most fortunate. If it were otherwise, the countries would fall to pieces. A reasonable view of modern nationalism is encouraged by going back to the world in which it developed. In the nineteenth century, every advanced European society faced a major political, economic, and social crisis. The French Revolution had undermined the old order everywhere, and it slowly became clear that conditions were such that it could not be repaired. The people were politically aroused to an unprecedented degree by the incendiary ideals of the Revolution and, later, by the new class ideologies of free trade and socialism. Economic life was in tumult from the new wealth and new misery of rapid industrial growth. Public administration broke down from the strain of a rapidly increasing urban population. The old political systems, often mortally weakened by the Revolution and its Napoleonic aftermath, could not cope with the new world. The task of creative politics was to find a political framework and constitutional formula within which the tumultuous new forces could be enticed into harmony and rational coordination. That formula was nationalism.[2] What, properly speaking, is nationalism?

Many writers define nationalism as a political disease—as the belief, held chiefly by elderly and benighted generals, that a national state may do as it pleases outside its borders and can rightfully demand unquestioning obedience from all citizens inside.[3] Such a definition is, of course, a crude caricature of nationalist theory which contributes little insight to the task of building political communities beyond the nation.

Nationalism might more properly be defined in its normal healthy, rather than occasionally diseased, form. It is that theory of the state which holds that political consensus can be achieved successfully only within the community of identity established by a *national* culture. Most nationalists by this definition have been quite reasonable people and it should be recognized that nationalism, whatever its present disadvantages, has been one of the great creative ideals in the modern world. The modern nation-state, as it has developed in Europe and America, is the most successful attempt so far in history to achieve peaceful democratic consensus within societies that are so vast, diverse, and politically conscious. It is difficult to imagine that modern democracy would have been possible without nationalism.

Naturally, the history of nationalist theory is complex. Nationalism was not a particular class ideology, but appealed to both left and right. There were innumerable theorists, each with his own particular concerns.[4] Most self-conscious theories of the nationalist state came as a reaction to the pretensions of one or another of the modern ideologies which claimed to be valid for all times, places, and cultures—Marxism, for example. Nationalism was characteristically the reaction of the culture which felt in danger of drowning, of being overwhelmed by some imperialistic and alien culture or ideology.

It is significant that Herder, the "father of nationalism," was inspired in the days before the French Revolution by the fear that the alien standards of French Classicism were smothering native German artistic vitality. Later German nationalists used Herder's ideas against Napoleon. Against the universal democratic pretensions of the French Revolution, conservative nationalists like Burke argued that each national culture had developed its characteristic institutions and traditions which could not be uprooted and replaced by some ideal construction without destroying both liberty and order.

Often the "alien" intrusion was an ideology with universal pretensions that threatened national cohesion by appealing to the special interests of some particular group in the society. Against Liberal *laissez faire,* British nationalist reformers like Coleridge and Disraeli argued for a positive government, both to provide for the welfare of the poorer classes and to uphold the traditional cultural values of the nation. Against Marxist class war, British Idealists like Bernard Bosanquet preached the reconciliation of classes around the concept of the larger interests of the national community.[5]

The nationalist was, of necessity, concerned with "consensus," that is, with achieving a degree of common identity and civic spirit that would rally the contentious elements of society towards rational cooperation with each other within an organized and generally accepted constitutional framework. Nationalism preoccupied itself with nourishing that common identity which was believed to spring from the common heritage of language, history, and culture—hence the whole panoply of nationalist symbols and ceremonies, the great emphasis on universal education, and often on universal military training as well. Monarchs or presidents, whatever their other functions, were made into symbols embodying national unity. Kings, emperors, and presidents thus acquired new prestige and, in the nineteenth century, there developed in some countries an unexpected affinity between monarchy and democracy.[6]

It is significant that modern democracy has almost never been established outside the context of a national state and that many later democratic theorists were also nationalists.[7] For the participation of the general populace in political power seemed to require that the people be imbued with some sense of civic duty, discipline, and responsibility. The more diverse the elements to be included, the more important it was that they share enough cultural homogeneity to understand each other and a deep common loyalty and identity which made it easier for them to defer to one another in the interest of the whole. Otherwise, representative democracy was thought to be impossible and the only hope for order was seen to be in an authoritarian rule based on governmental force and popular indifference. Nationalism, of course, appealed to conservatives as well as democrats.[8] Traditionalist leaders who were unenthusiastic about democracy often came to realize that a growing measure of popular participation in government was unavoidable and that only nationalism could keep these elements from tearing apart the traditional structure. In England, Disraeli's Tories became partisans of nationalist empire and democratic suffrage, and, as a result, benefited from strong lower class support.

Nation-building in the broadest sense—achieving a synthesis of old and new forms, reconciling the social classes to each other's claims, gaining organized control of the elements of economic, social, and political life—was the major preoccupation throughout the nineteenth century, not only of the new states nationalism had called into being, but of the old states it sought to preserve.

While the national state was successfully bringing order and coordination to domestic politics and society, it was preparing the ground for international chaos of unparalleled destructiveness. For nationalism, however indispensable its contribution to modern constitutional democratic government, has shown itself to possess two dangerous tendencies: domestically, it tends towards the concentration of power; internationally, it promotes instability and conflict.

Inside the nation, the continual emphasis on national interest tended to give more and more power to the government. While both liberal and conservative nationalists often stressed the virtues of regional diversity and local government, the attempt to check central power was successful only in nations like England and the United States with strong local traditions. In France, however, Jacobin nationalism was itself highly centralist and only reinforced the dangerous overcentralization inherited from the monarchy. It is not surprising that much of the federalist reaction to centralization should spring from France.[9]

Nationalism's second inherent difficulty was its necessary view of international relations. The ideal of a sovereign political community, organized within a national context, led by definition to an uncoordinated world order where war was always a possibility. Most nationalist theorists frankly accepted the inevitability of occasional war in a contentious world where conflict could not be eliminated altogether.[10] In common with most of mankind, nationalists tended to deplore the suffering and waste of war, but also were impressed by the nobler sentiments of courage, duty, and sacrifice which war inspired among citizens. Some, under Darwinist influence, saw war as the test by which those societies which had successfully achieved a high degree of consensus triumphed over those weakened by their own internal contradictions.[11] War rewarded the successful and eliminated the unfit. For most nationalists, however, war was initially an inevitable evil, but was likely to disappear as states progressively resolved their inner social and political tensions. As nations grew more at peace with themselves, they would be more at peace with their neighbors and less eager to hazard their internal achievements in international adventures.[12]

The present disrepute of nationalism springs from a heightened awareness of its dangerous propensities rather than from any notable enthusiasm for its alternatives. It is not surprising that after the terrible slaughter of the world wars and with nuclear weapons in prospect, the traditional nationalist complacency towards war seems outrageous. After our experiences with totalitarianism, we are frightened of a system that encourages strong emotional loyalty to a central government. Moreover, the terrible lesson of history has been that the two dangerous tendencies of nationalism are complementary and reinforcing.

Nationalism sought to bring under control the vast new energies within modern society. War on the outside often seemed an easy way to build unity inside. It was always easier to define the national interest in the face of a common enemy. The thorny problems of industrial and social relations could be resolved or deferred in the midst of a great national military crusade. Meanwhile, the immense new power that nationalism had harnessed raised war to colossal proportions and, indeed, brought warfare back to a scale of destructive barbarism suggested by the Revolution and Napoleon but not really seen in Europe since the seventeenth century wars of religion.

When the sport of kings became the frenzy of peoples, war easily grew to fulfill the terrible promise of the Revolution and Napoleon. Both the policies of governments and the means employed grew so extravagant that they defied any rational calculation of gains and losses. With World War I, the war of nations, modern warfare passed beyond all previous measure. Not only was the carnage in itself stupefying, but the resultant economic and emotional disruption threatened to overturn, in country after country, the whole domestic social order that nationalism had painfully managed to create. Though it might be questionable whether Hitler's totalitarian, racist doctrines should be called nationalism at all, the whole phenomenon of Nazism did grow out of the utter demoralization which nationalist war had brought to Germany, and did illustrate in a spectacular fashion the twin dangers of a world order of national states—too much control within nations and too little without.[13]

2.

Not surprisingly, among those who climbed out of the rubble of World War II, there was widespread resolution that the European national states should never be allowed another opportunity to demonstrate their disastrous propensities. The idea of unified Europe enjoyed one of its periodic revivals; calls for a new European order came from many quarters, and a large and enthusiastic federalist movement became a prominent feature of the postwar political scene.

Federalism, like nationalism, is a complex movement containing a great variety of writers with highly individual concerns. It has become fashionable to define federalism as a process—the process by which the power to make decisions passes from the central government of states either to some new center beyond the nation or to regional authorities within it. A noted student of federalism, Carl Friedrich, defines it as:

> . . . *either* the process by which a number of separate political organizations, be they states or any other kind of association, enter into arrangements for working out solutions together, that is to say adopting joint policies and making joint decisions on common problems, *or* the process through which a hitherto unitarily organized political community, as it becomes differentiated into a number of separate and distinct political subcommunities, achieves a new order in which the differentiated communities, now separately organized, become capable of working out separately and on their own those solutions they no longer have in common.[14]

Federalism, however, is not only an observable process, but also the political ideal which has been nationalism's chief competitor in the world of political philosophy. There is a long federalist tradition going back several centuries in the West and embracing many diverse schools of writers. All, in one way or another, opposed the predominant European pattern of independent centralized states.[15] Federalist philosophy has concerned itself with setting forth its ideal, the federalist community, and, in modern times, with explaining why such a community is both a desirable and possible alternative to nationalism.

After the terrible holocaust of World War I had illustrated the disadvantages of the nationalist order, it was only natural that federalist ideas should receive increasing popular attention in Europe. A wide variety were publicized from diverse sources. In the 1920's, Count Richard Coudenhove-Kalergi founded an important group, Pan-Europa, which skillfully disseminated federalist ideas among Europe's political, economic, and cultural elites.[16] In 1929, the French foreign minister, Aristide Briand, working closely with his German counterpart, Gustave Stresemann, formally introduced a project for a European confederation. In the discouraging years of the 1930's, a distinguished school of writers, the Personalists, advocated a thorough recasting along federalist lines of the internal structure of the nation-states as the means for avoiding the totalitarian tendencies of modern mass society.[17] Just before the war, Clarence Streit wrote his influential *Union Now* which attacked the League of Nations for its weakness and called for an Atlantic federal government with enough real power to make a new war impossible.[18] The Second World War increased sentiment against the nation-state. The public was electrified in 1940 by Churchill's spectacular offer to merge the British and French governments.[19] Theorists of the Resistance, perhaps most especially in Italy, were strongly attracted to federalism.[20]

The end of the war in Europe began a period of intense interest in federalist ideas. Churchill and de Gaulle both launched confederal schemes. Committees were organized to spread federalist ideas among business interests and national political parties.[21] Numerous meetings were held and innumerable manifestoes spread about. In 1946, theorists of all schools joined together to discuss their ideas in the European Union of Federalists. In May, 1948, partisans of a new order assembled at The Hague in a great Congress of Europe. Churchill and Adenauer headed a list of over six hundred delegates who roared their approval as speaker after speaker called on Europe to unite.[22] In short, there was no lack of acquaintance with federalist ideas. There was, in addition, evangelical enthusiasm and great conviction that the nation-state was no longer by itself a sufficient framework for organizing the political, economic, social, and cultural forces of the modern world. However, in spite of several years of intense federalist speculation there was little agreement on what form the new Europe should take or on how it should be achieved. The divisions, in fact, were broad and sharp.

To some extent the lack of agreement sprang from contradictions in the federalist movement itself. Federalism clearly has had two distinct if not contradictory aims. These separate aims have in turn resulted in two distinct groupings of postwar federalists —on the one hand, the confederalists and the constitutionalists who are mostly concerned with international unity, and, on the other, the integralists who are primarily interested in domestic reform.

The aim of the confederal and constitutional groups, union at the top, is a familiar cause in Western political theory. Schemes for confederation have appeared regularly throughout European history. Generally they call for formal machinery to coordinate the policies and forces of a group of powers who have agreed to act together to prevent international aggression and conflict. More recent confederal proposals have often stressed additional common aims, especially economic development. Churchill had a confederation in mind in the early days after the war. NATO is a confederation, as would be General de Gaulle's Europe of States. Unions remain confederal rather than federal as long as members may lawfully refuse to follow the decisions of the group as a whole.

Those who favor a more intense federal union have often argued that confederations are effective only when one member is strong enough to compel the others to follow.[23] While Russia might be said to have established a successful confederation in Eastern Europe, and while NATO can be expected to hold together as a confederation as long as the United States is militarily so powerful and the Russian threat remains, no purely Western European confederation could be expected to work because there is no one power big enough to overawe the others. True, Western Europeans have many interests in common, but as long as each state is free to withdraw at will, the union will suffer from the difficulty so trenchantly cited long ago by Rousseau:

It will perhaps be said that society is so formed that every man gains by serving the rest. That would be all very well, if he did not gain still more by injuring them. There is no legitimate profit so great, that it cannot be greatly exceeded by what may be made illegitimately; we always gain more by hurting our neighbors than by doing them good.[24]

In short, the militant federalist, from Alexander Hamilton to Clarence Streit to Altiero Spinelli, has had no faith in the durability of confederations. For a union to become a reality, there must be federal institutions with real power over states, power that does not depend on the consent of the governments of those states.

There is always the problem of where the federal power is to come from. It cannot be decreed by well-meaning reformers. In modern Western democracies, political power is based on popular consent. If a federal government is to have the preponderant power in a federation, it must find some means to capture the loyalty of the people. To do so, the federal authority will have to employ the devices by which loyalty is cultivated within the present national states. But if the federal power is successful, it will, in fact, have turned the federation into something similar in many important ways to a national state.[25] This, at least, has been the American pattern. The federalizing process, to succeed, must continue until a new nation is formed.

That is what some European federalists clearly want: a United States of Europe with a supreme federal government chosen democratically. The chief difference between these constitutional federalists and the nationalists lies in their differing views on the possibility of obtaining a sufficient consensus for unity. While a nationalist would argue that a community the size of Europe would be too diverse for a working political consensus, the federalist would probably counter with the old argument from Hamilton that increasing the "orbit" of government actually increases political stability.[26] Europe united would be more stable than most of its parts taken separately. In a united Europe, for example, no single undemocratic clique could hope to seize power in a sudden *coup d'état*. There would be immense new economic potential. Parliamentary politics would revive as new European parties would have to be formed around real new issues and could shed the futile heritage of the past century's ideological battles.

Nevertheless, many constitutional federalists agree that any European federal government would have to be very strong and enjoy enormous prestige to counter, especially in a democracy, the centrifugal tendencies in so diverse a community as Europe.

But the building of a strong central power is a program which carries this constitutional school far away from the second main group of federalists, the integralists, whose chief aim is to break up centralized bureaucratic power and to replace it with a wide variety of regional and local authorities. This strain in federalism, provoked by nationalism's domestic rather than international shortcomings, descends from a long corporatist tradition including such writers as Althusius, the seventeenth century Dutch opponent of monarchical centralization, and Proudhon, the nineteenth century French socialist anarchist, and embracing some modern Catholic social and political theory as well.

It is the tradition which seems the most removed from the nationalist preoccupation with consensus. It is a school opposed not so much to the nation as to the state. In the eyes of unsympathetic critics, the integral federalists hanker for a sort of preindustrial utopia in which the facts of our highly centralized modern world are somehow annulled. Power is meant to be so lost in an elaborate network of local arrangements that the would-be dictator can never find it.

The more reasonable modern federalists influenced by this school, Henri Brugmans for example, do not deny the need for consensus and coordinating leadership in a federal society. But for Brugmans, cultural variety is an end in itself: the best society is that which enjoys just this kind of diversity. He does not deny the nationalist assumption that to maintain such a society requires a high degree of consensus, "entente" as he calls it, as well as vigorous political leadership to keep ahead of the problems that are potentially divisive. Brugmans purports not to be opposed to power as such, but only to government that crushes individuality and initiative. The misuse of power, he argues, is best guarded against not by anarchy, the absence of any effective power anywhere, but by a multiplicity of powers, each strong within a circumscribed sphere. Government, therefore, should be divided into various areas—the "spaces of federalism"—within which there is a public authority, responsible to its constituents and adequately empowered to come to grips with the problems which legitimately fall within its responsibility. The boundaries of the constituencies should be determined by the scope of particular problems—municipal for town planning and "Atlantic" for defense.[27]

There is, needless to say, a strong bias for any unit—supranational or regional—that would cut across present national boundaries. According to Brugmans, many national boundaries are highly arbitrary divisions of natural economic and cultural units. If Europe were liberated from the nation-state, natural regions long submerged would reassert themselves and become effective contexts for vigorous planning and growth.[28]

Brugmans agrees that planning is essential and that local plans must always be subject to a broader view from above. But initiative should come from below, he argues, from numerous regional and professional groups and interests. The higher authority should only "orchestrate" the plans from below. To the unconvinced, any drastic dispersion of power would seem to run counter to the whole trend of modern affairs—including that logic of economic and military interdependence which is counted on to lead the nations of Europe into a federation. Skeptics may wonder if personal freedom fares best in small communities. The belief that local government is generally stupid government is not altogether unsupported by evidence.

But for Brugmans and his school, federalism as he defines it is essential to the survival of Western democracy and he warns that only by breaking the vast, alien, secretive bureaucracies of the national states, only by the cultivation of local responsibility and initiative, can there be a renewal of the sagging morale of Western civilization. And only by such a renewal can the West gain the spiritual vitality and confidence to resist the totalitarianism implicit in modern mass society.

The causes for tension between the two wings of the European federalists should be apparent. It is as if Hamilton and Jefferson were in the same political party. They can coexist, as we know in America, but the eventual price may be civil war. Indeed, the conflict between the two groups of European federalists did, in 1956, finally break up the Union of European Federalists.

In spite of their differences, many federalists, particularly those who stem from the last generation, seem to share a common attitude in one most important respect. They are not fascinated, indeed they are repelled, by international power politics. In contrast to de Gaulle, who frankly accepts the need for conflict, heroism, and sacrifice in international life, the federalists long for a world in which great international contests and adventures are somehow forbidden. They want Europe united, not to contend for grandeur with America and Russia, but so that a larger garden can be cultivated more efficiently. Their model is Switzerland. Above all, they are frightened of political institutions which cater to personal prestige. They want their monarchs to be figureheads. They may want a European Parliament, but are generally uninterested in a European President. They would prefer their executive, like the Swiss, to be a commission. They prefer government by committee. They are aristocratic republicans and they see no need for a king. Thus they deplore Gaullism and the whole tendency in modern national states towards the "personalization of power." [29] When told that a European union without a strong presidential executive would be unable to play an active role in world politics, they are not much disturbed. The typical federalist is often prepared to leave these matters to

America. It is what de Gaulle, in scorn, calls "the philosophy of letting-go." For the average federalist, it is common sense and civilization.

The federalist theorists have contributed much to the European movement, but for the moment they are not its active leaders. Direction of the campaign for unity has passed to the functionalists, to the Eurocrats of the Common Market. They share many federalist ideas, but they are not so much philosophers and writers as successful men of affairs—bureaucrats and businessmen. They are the men, like Jean Monnet and Walter Hallstein, who have inspired and run the European Communities. Out of their experiences in those groups, they have gradually developed a theory purporting to show how the present supranational institutions can successfully evolve into a new type of federal government.

While the role of federalist theorists in the European movement has seemingly declined in recent years, the importance of federalist theory, like nationalist, does not depend on a specific set of proposals drawn from a particular writer. The ideals of both nationalist and federalist philosophy reflect broad ways of looking at the whole problem of organizing a political community. Both movements contribute to the general arsenal of ideas within which statesmen find new schemes for bringing order to their rapidly changing world. Most practical proposals today will probably be found to have both nationalist and federalist elements. Yet the two movements are fundamentally opposed to each other over the question of what constitutes a desirable and possible political community. In the background of today's battle in Europe over the grand alternatives, there is a very old struggle in the world of ideas which, in one way or another, has perhaps gone on since the beginning of politics.

While federalism as an ideal has gained many ardent enthusiasts in modern times, federalism as a process seeking to convert the national states into a new order has made little progress. In such contests, nationalism has invariably triumphed. A federalizing Europe would be set on a path towards a common government which would eventually put an end to the political independence of the present national states. The nations of Europe have never before been willing to accept such a renunciation of their freedom, regardless of the inconveniences of independence. History has seen other attempts at European unity, but they have all foundered. Why should this last one succeed?

History seems to repeat itself more often in Europe than elsewhere. The politics of Europe have often seemed a game of chess, played with highly individualistic pieces but limited by its framework to a number of recurring patterns. Yet it is also probable that, since the last war, the game has changed. The present drive to unity has taken place against a background of unusual conditions which may just possibly lead to a break from the old patterns.

The war's end found the national states of Europe in a condition of unparalleled weakness and demoralization. European states soon discovered that they could not possibly resume their old positions of world power. Their empires gradually slipped away. Indeed, they could not even begin to defend themselves at home against the imminent threat of communist domination. If sovereignty meant autonomy, then national sovereignty had become an illusion, for no European nation had the strength to play an independent role. In short, the terrible weakness of all the European powers, even victorious Britain, made some sort of coalition seem only natural.

The nation-state was supposed to be finished. Economically, politically and militarily, it was the age of superstates. In those days, even de Gaulle believed that "we are in an age of concentration."[30] Under the circumstances, a great many normally patriotic Europeans found old-fashioned national patriotism reactionary. Instead, nationalism was itself blamed for Europe's decline. It was Hitler's nationalism that had plunged Europe into ruinous war; it was nationalism which stood in the way of the federation that was Europe's last hope. While these postwar sentiments may have been strongest in the defeated countries where the prospect of a purely national renewal seemed unimaginable, they were widespread in England and France as well. The heady idealism of European unity had not only more support but less resistance than ever before.

The aggrandizement of Russia had reduced Europe to only half its normal size, and that in itself simplified the task of harmonizing interests. Communist imperialism obviously provoked cohesion among its intended victims. Free Europe was driven together not only by a common fear, but by a common dependence upon the United States, without whose constant protection it would soon have been overrun. American protection imposed conditions which were in themselves an unusual incentive to European unity. The United States insisted first that economic and then military support be channeled through international organizations within which the Europeans planned together their economic revival and military defense. As a result of their experiences in the Organization of European Economic Cooperation and NATO, by the time they came to create organizations of their own, the European governments had already progressed far in the habits and techniques necessary to make intergovernmental machinery function smoothly.[31]

Unification was made easier, not only by the division of Europe as a whole, but in particular by the division of Germany. It can be argued that almost all the postwar progress towards unity has depended on Germany's partition, for it is hardly conceivable that the Western communities could ever have achieved such a degree of integration if Germany had been at her full size.[32] Germany united is too large, too populous, and too powerful to be fitted peacefully within the European framework.[33] While Germany has never succeeded in imposing lasting hegemony over the rest of Europe, it has taken the combined power of Britain, America, and Russia to stop her. But Western Germany, while still richer and potentially more powerful than her neighbors, is cut down to a size which enables her to become an equal partner of France and allays the fears that would normally paralyze European cooperation. Furthermore, the Germans' relative weakness and high vulnerability made them eager to find friends in the West, indeed to escape from intolerable guilt by finding a new identity for themselves in Europe.

Germany's convenient partition has, moreover, seemed likely to last indefinitely, since it was for a great many people one of the few beneficial results of the Second World War. It is difficult to see how any relevant national interest will lead to reunification in the near future. It is not in the interest of the rest of Western Europe, at least until there is some tight Western European political union to contain the Germans. Most important of all, it is unlikely to be in Russia's interest until perhaps the prospect of a powerful, united, Western European state or nuclear Atlantic Alliance seems so imminent and alarming that the Soviets play their ultimate trump card and offer the Germans reunification if they will renounce the West. Even then, what would the Russians be likely to consider worse, a federal Western Europe with all the internal balances that might well keep such a grouping from too adventurous a policy, or a powerful Germany, suffering from internal indigestion but free from the constraints imposed by membership in a federation with several timid neighbors?

It is the Russians who hold the key. Their allies who possess former German territory are not likely to be enthusiastic for reunification, nor is the East German regime itself. The United States supports reunification in principle, but it is difficult to see what steps the American government could or would take to bring it about. We are unlikely, in the short run at least, to favor German or European disarmament or neutrality. General de Gaulle's Europe from the Atlantic to the Urals is meant for the future. In short, Germany is likely to remain divided and its division facilitates greatly the task of bringing Western Europe into voluntary union.

The drastically changed world position of Britain is yet another unusual feature favoring unity in postwar Europe. Traditionally the British have always opposed attempts at Continental unity. And for centuries, they have gazed with disapproval upon what seemed the instability, tyranny, and peculiar habits of the Continentals. Success appeared to justify their confidence. They alone of the Western Europeans suffered neither ignominious defeat nor shamefaced victory in the last war. At its end, they had less reason than most to doubt the adequacy of their old habits and values. Nevertheless, there was considerable pro-European and antinationalist sentiment in Britain. Churchill for a while led the European movement. British governments, however, were always tepid and sometimes openly hostile.

But the intervening years have been cruel for Britain. The British are a people used to greatness. The resigned acceptance of an increasingly minor place, however admirably mature, is not likely to be the best solution for them or for the rest of the world. The logic of events seems to be pushing England into Europe. It has taken a long time for that logic to impress itself on the British government. The British have missed many opportunities to join, indeed to lead Europe. When the decision to join the Common Market finally came, it seemed so conditional and so precariously based that its failure should not have been altogether surprising. But nothing has shown better the strong pull of European unity on Britain than the change in the attitude of the Socialists since they have come to power. The education of the Socialists may be time well spent. The next British bid to join Europe should be less ambiguous and have more the character of a genuine and stable expression of national will. Such an offer would be far more difficult to resist for Britain has too much to give Europe, both politically and economically. That England should be considering such a future is itself a major change in the traditional European pattern.

Finally, the postwar European scene has been radically changed by the presence of supranational communities—above all the Common Market. The dream of Europe has settled into concrete institutions, headed by a most able and imaginative group of functionaries with powerful connections in government, business, the press, and the universities—functionaries who exercise real powers with great skill over an increasing area of European life. Those who have sought to find a new organization to replace the national state have realized a major practical achievement. The practical experience and theory of these Communities is priceless capital for the European movement. If the theories of the functionalists are a rather penurious extract from the riches of federalist philosophy, in any event the functionalists have escaped from the garrulous futility to which visionaries have usually been condemned. They have begun the "process."

The new institutionalized European power, together with the radically changed European political chessboard, makes an eventual European community a good deal more probable than it has ever been in the past. In postwar Europe, federalism may at last be beginning a career as a process. It is against this not altogether unpromising background that the major proposals for a European union, the latest contest between nationalism and federalism, must be considered.

The Common Market's Federalist Europe

III.

The Common Market's Federalist Europe

Out of the broad federalist and functionalist movement has evolved the most radical of the grand alternatives, the supranational Europe of the Common Market.[1] Today, Europe is no longer only an idea, but an institution—a political community which not only disposes of formidable and ever-growing power, but which already possesses the basic structure necessary to form the government of a new European federal state. That, at least, is the claim made frequently by Dr. Walter Hallstein, President of the Commission of the European Economic Community (the Common Market).[2]

If some find the claim exaggerated, nearly all agree that the achievement has been extraordinary. Europe's economies have made steady progress towards unity. Numerous expected pitfalls have been avoided and seemingly insoluble conflicts resolved. The whole enterprise has been, in fact, a brilliant and sustained *tour de force* illustrating, it would seem, how skillful modern administration can be in guiding events to avoid conflict and promote general solidarity. By projecting their impressive success into the future, the supranational communities have laid their claim to become the government of that federal Europe they have been so confident of bringing about. Whatever their ultimate fate, the supranational communities have posed an ideal that has appealed to many powerful interests, inspired a large section of enlightened opinion, and permanently affected the drive to unite Europe. To understand this ideal and its prospects, it is important to have answers for five basic questions:

First, how has the Common Market, an economic community, developed into the institution which carries with it the hope for a federal Europe?

Second, what is the Common Market's present structure?

Third, how is that structure meant to transform itself into the government of Europe?

Fourth, what are its prospects for doing so?

Fifth, and finally, what are the fundamental assumptions and beliefs of the partisans of this particular grand alternative?

1.

The present supranational communities are the culmination of a number of postwar experiments.[3] The movement to gather the states of Europe into a larger community passed into an institutional phase around 1949. Its several institutions and proposals can be classified in a number of different ways: first, as to whether they embrace the whole North Atlantic area, are limited to Western Europe, or are further limited to the Six—Belgium, France, Germany, Italy, Luxembourg, and the Netherlands. NATO (1949) covers the North Atlantic; the Council of Europe (1949), nearly all Western Europe; the Coal and Steel Community (1950), Euratom and the Common Market (1958), only the Six.

These institutions can also be classified as confederal or federal. NATO and the Council of Europe are confederations. The Communities of the Six are more intensely federal in their structure. Members are bound by decisions which will eventually be taken by a majority,[4] and each has a supranational bureaucracy.[5] The classification suggests the important issues in the drive to create a federal community for the nations of Europe. Basically, there have been three issues: size, scope, and organization.

Events since the War have given at least a provisional settlement to each. The first issue, size, depended on the attitude of the United States and Britain. While the United States has pushed its various Atlantic arrangements, particularly the military integration of NATO, it has not, at least until recently, been worried by conflict between "Atlantic partnership" and European unity. Indeed, America has generally seen the two aims as complementary. Only a strong Europe could be the second "pillar" of the Alliance and enter into a real partnership of power and responsibility with America.[6] Thus for many years, America has openly championed a separate European union within a larger Atlantic community. The size of that separate European union has turned mainly on whether Britain would join.

The European unionists were eager from the beginning to include England. The first of the major European institutions, the Council of Europe, was watered down to soothe the Labor Government's opposition to any pooling of national sovereignty. Once inside, the British government became a continual drag on the progress of the Council, and indeed, if there is any single cause for the disappointing performance of that institution, it has been the presence of Britain within it.. Britain's behavior was naturally a great disappointment to anyone seriously interested in European unity, including many of the British themselves.[7]

In their discouragement, the partisans of Europe began to think of building a union without Britain. The main stumbling block was the reconciliation of France and Germany. Without England as a comrade, the French were wary of arrangments that tied them tightly to Germany. But since their alliance with England was disappointing, the French began to face coming to terms with their dangerous neighbors. At this point, two Frenchmen long devoted to the European cause, Robert Schuman, the Foreign Minister, and Jean Monnet, the "Father of Europe," produced what must surely be one of the most imaginative diplomatic solutions in modern history, the European Coal and Steel Community.[9] It was impossible, they argued, to tie together France and Germany through classical diplomatic arrangements. The basic problem was that neither could afford to concede much to the other without feeling its own security and prosperity endangered, and thus the old cycle of competition and fear had continued endlessly. The only solution was to fuse the two countries in such a way that each would lose its independent power to do mortal harm to the other. They could then cooperate without fearing that what benefited one invariably threatened the other.

The solution, the Coal and Steel Community, proposed placing the coal and steel industries, vital to war making, under a supranational authority not dominated by any national government. Adenauer's Germany was delighted with the plan. The rest of Western Europe was invited to join and Italy and Benelux soon did. It is interesting that the four continental ministers who played a critical role in establishing the Coal and Steel Community—Adenauer, Beck, de Gasperi, and Schuman—were each Catholic Christian Democrats, came from a border area of mixed nationality, and were fluent in German.[10]

The British hesitated, equivocated, and finally refused. A

change in government had brought no change in European policy. Out of office, it is true, Churchill was the father of Europe, but once back in power he did little to legitimize his Continental offspring.[11] Europe went on without England. The Franco-German axis was formed and the Europe of the Six was born.

The pattern repeated itself in the next major initiative towards European unity, the European Defense Community. The Korean War had made Washington eager to rearm Germany. It was hoped that the same supranational arrangement would neutralize the danger to Europe of the German rearmament which American pressure had made imminent. The European Defense Treaty was proposed by René Pleven, the French Foreign Minister, in September, 1950, and ratified by all the Six except France.

The stakes in EDC were very high. To have persuaded the national states to renounce their independent military power and place it under the control of a supranational agency would obviously have been a most decisive step towards a federal Europe. The Treaty openly called for the establishment of a federal or confederal European government based on the separation of powers to coordinate all the Communities within a common political structure.[12] Quite apart from the formal proposals, a common army would probably have demanded rapid political integration, since some sort of strong political authority would have been essential to control the immense power of a centralized European military establishment. Common military policy would seemingly have required a common foreign policy, and, because military expenditures play such a vital role in economic life, probably a common fiscal policy as well. In short, if a common army had been created, a central government with significant power would have followed almost inevitably. The shrewder partisans and opponents of the measure were well aware of its significance.

Five of the Six agreed, but Britain refused. Eden's policy caused much resentment among good Europeans. Paul-Henri Spaak, president of the Consultative Assembly of the Council of

Europe, resigned after an angry speech drawing what was, for him, a sad conclusion: to try to build a Europe based on England would be to renounce Europe. The Council of Europe, tailored to meet British requirements, was ample proof of the kind of Europe Britain would accept. Clearly there was not sufficient harmony in a greater Europe for the attainment of close unity.[13] In Spaak's view, the Continent would have to proceed towards federation on its own.

The European Army required too much integration, not only for the English but for the French as well. It may be true that if Britain had joined, France would have followed. Britain's presence might have soothed French fears of German militarism and relieved French doubts that the plan was a subtle Anglo-Saxon manuever to deprive France of the means to hold on to her empire. But after the British refusal, France, had it joined, would have been the only large power to give up national control of its army. Germany still had no army and there was no possibility, of course, that the United States would give up national control. In short, with Britain in, at least the French would not have been able to find so many convenient excuses for staying out. But England was even less willing to give up her independence than France. Without England or France to balance Germany, a European Defense Community was of course impossible. The battle for a European federation took place in the French Assembly, and in August, 1954, the battle was lost.[14]

The whole episode not only strengthened the belief of the federalists that they would have to proceed without Britain, but it settled for the moment the question of what the scope of the European institutions could be. A strictly European defense organization was out. For the foreseeable future, the military integration of Western Europe would take place only within an American-dominated NATO. Their failure answered the second great question confronting the unionists. Their bold and direct attempt to set up a federal state had failed. They became, by necessity, gradualists and functionalists. The era of broad schemes for federal constitutions was over. The French coal and steel industries could be federalized, but not the French army. If political integration was to come about at all, it was to be through the gradual extension of supranational control in economic matters.[15] It was hoped that economic federalization, once started, would "spill over" from one field to the next.

If the good Europeans were to be limited to the economic sphere, they resolved to make the best of it. Proposals for a Common Market came within a year after the defeat of the European Defense Community, and by 1957 the governments of the Six had pledged themselves to create a common economy.[16]

Once again the British reponse was negative. This time, the British not only refused to participate in the Community but tried to wreck it. The British government proposed a general European free-trade area, involving neither supranational machinery nor any commitment to general economic integration. The British proposals were bitterly opposed by the Common Market Commission. In its opinion, England sought "to benefit from the advantages of the Community without making any of the sacrifices."[17]

The free-trade area was a mortal threat to the Commission's aims. Those who composed the Common Market were chiefly interested in the creation of a common European economy. Such a common economy was impossible, they believed, unless strong measures were taken throughout the member countries to create uniform conditions of competition. Governments would have to renounce granting special subsidies or imposing their own import quotas. Capital and workers would have to be able to move freely within the market and there would have to be a common tariff on raw materials and other goods from without. Weak economies, like the Italian, would need special aid to catch up with the strong; otherwise free trade would merely aid the domination of the weak by the strong. Countries like Germany and Holland, though partisans of free trade by interest and inclination, accepted the principle that the merger of their economies with those of their weaker and more protectionist neighbors would require extensive planning and careful management. Britain refused to cede so much economic control. Those countries which had signed the Treaty of Rome were again left no choice but to continue by themselves. Britain, meanwhile, created the European Free Trade Association and Europe was formally divided into "Sixes and Sevens."

Thus by 1959 events had settled, at least for the time being, the first two issues confronting the European movement. It was a Europe of Six and its integration had begun in the economic sphere. The third issue, its organization, had found a provisional solution in the unique supranational pattern of the European "Communities," an ingenious arrangement involving both federal and confederal elements.

2.

A great deal has been written about the unique organization of the European Communities.[18] They are a blend of national and supranational elements which makes their structure unlike that of any national state. There is the Council of Ministers to represent the national governments, the Commission made up of supranational functionaries, the European Parliament with delegates chosen by the national parliaments, and the High Court of Justice. In classic terms, the Commission is the executive, the Council the legislature, and the Court the judiciary. The European Parliament serves as a forum to draw out and focus public opinion but has little role in legislation.

Policies result from a complex dialogue between the Council and the Commission. It is the Council which has the final say and, until 1966 at least, each member state has a veto. On the other hand, the Commission has substantial political powers of its own aside from its inevitable strength as the chief administrator of policies once they are made. The Commission, for example, has great influence over the substance of Council debates. In most matters, only the Commission can initiate and formulate the actual proposals before the Council—a power which gives the Commission, among other things, a formal veto in the Council.[19]

Furthermore, the Commission is reasonably independent. The Treaty insists that Commission members not be subject to instructions from their own governments and that they be appointed for long terms. Many are high civil servants of recognized ability and substance in their own countries.[20] There is every indication that their personal independence has in fact been respected. They may not be in a position to take an intransigently hostile attitude towards the national governments—a determined government could probably destroy the position of any member of the Commission—but on the other hand, a Commissioner with such a provocative disposition would not contribute much to the Commission's work, for its chief role is that of an inspired mediator, coaxing the national states into agreement.[21]

It is generally agreed that the extraordinary progress of the Common Market would have been impossible without the supranational Commission.[22] As an institutionalized mediator with independent powers of initiative, it has often acted in Council debates as a catalyst, inspiring decisions that do in fact seem to represent a common European interest rather than an old-fashioned diplomatic compromise of separate and conflicting national aims. The Commission's role is self-consciously political rather than merely technical. It has actively sought to embody the "European" interest in the Council. Its identity with Europe makes it easier for the national governments to give in to the Commission than to one another. Altruism is more popular at home than appeasement. It is easier for Frenchmen to make sacrifices to Europe than to Germany.[23]

The successes of the Commission, of course, are possible only because of the active cooperation of the national governments. Economic integration has not in reality come about through technocratic magic. A great many problems are completely insoluble on a technical level and in many issues diplomatic charm cannot mask the brutal truth that someone must lose. Agriculture is perhaps the most notable example. The best way to block agreement on such issues is to leave negotiations to technical experts alone. Solutions come only after politicians decide that the general advantages of agreement are worth the cost to their particular national interests. Only the states can make that decision. While the independent mediating role of the Commission has been a necessary condition of the success of the enterprise, it would not have been sufficient if the states had lost their fundamental will to pay the necessary costs to create a common European economy.

Writers on the Common Market have perhaps tended to place too much emphasis on the role of the Commission and not enough on that of the Council itself. The preoccupation is understandable. Among the Commission's skills, public relations is not the least. Furthermore, the Commission is a genuine institutional novelty and hence of great interest to the professional student. But it is at least as great a novelty that six European governments have sustained for so many years so constant a devotion to the success of an international institution which enters into a vital area of their national life. Given that will, it has been possible for the Commission to find a way.

Particularly striking is the degree to which, in a number of the most critical issues, the position of the French government has been close to that of the Commission. Indeed, it is quite possible to argue that, of all the national governments, it is de Gaulle's France which has supported most vigorously and constantly the first aim of the Rome Treaty, the creation of a genuinely integrated European economy.[24] It is obvious that similar policies can have quite different ends in view.[25] De Gaulle, in spite of his crucial and indeed indispensable aid to the specific goal of the Rome Treaty, economic integration, has a more dubious claim to being the chief supporter of the ultimate purpose of that treaty, political integration. He shares not at all the Commission's avowed aim of transforming the present supranational communities into a federal governing structure for Europe. Nevertheless, de Gaulle, in following his own purposes, has made it possible for the European Economic Community to advance far along the way towards the creation of a European economy. The question is whether in doing so he has unwittingly also advanced the cause of eventual political unity under the same supranational arrangements. That, of course, is the crucial question. Though the Commission's official view is perhaps more cautious, many who expect European union to grow out of the Common Market believe that economic integration will in itself almost inevitably lead to political union.[26]

The basis for the confident hopes of the faithful is the so-called "spill-over effect" which has become the cherished theory—it might almost be said the ideology—of the avid partisans of the Common Market. Economic integration is believed to have an irresistible inner logic, as stated succinctly by the President of the Common Market Commission, Walter Hallstein: "Like the alphabet, all economic policy has an inner unity which is stronger than any arbitrary action of political powers."[27] The federalizing tendencies of economic union will spill over into politics until national governments finally will have ceded so much of their power that European unity will have occurred in fact before it is conceded in principle. " 'Political' integration is not a condition of economic integration but its consequence."[28] What are the basic tenets of this sanguine theory, the ideology of the Common Market?

3.

The whole process by which the Common Market has worked towards integrating the Six into a common economy has been carefully studied with an eye to determining the inner logic of that process and the conditions that have helped or hindered it. There have been several attempts to formulate a general theory purporting to spell out the conditions which enable an international organization to become the nucleus for the eventual political integration of its members. Political integration is seen as the process by which member states give up making key public policies independently and instead make them jointly within a supranational cadre or pass them on to a new supranational administration.[29]

Under the right conditions, it is said, the federalizing process of moving decisions to a new center accelerates from an inherent dynamism. As the new center gains importance, significant individuals and groups in society shift their attention and activities towards it.[30] And with this shifting of attention and activity, new loyalties and allegiances are gradually developed. Up to a certain point, even conflicts among members are thought to hasten integration. Experience indicates that the most generally acceptable solution is that which can claim to be "in the Community interest." Such solutions generally result in a fresh delegation of power to the new center.[31]

The whole integrating process, it is said, can take place quite apart from forces in the world of ideas and general public opinion. Thus, under the right conditions, there is felt to be in the process itself an internal dynamism which hurries it along faster the farther it has gone.[32]

What are thought to be the right conditions? To begin with, the institutions which develop policies must actually exist. The importance of their tasks must be recognized if they are to stir up significant social and economic forces within the separate countries. The tasks, in addition, must be inherently expansive and thus tend to increase the role of the new central institutions. Finally, if the dynamism is to continue, the member states must continue to see their interests as consistent with the whole supranational enterprise. If these conditions exist, then it can be expected that there will be an inner push towards greater and greater concentration of power, attention, and loyality towards the new center. Do these general theories of integration apply to the Common Market?

Obviously, and not surprisingly, they do. Elaborate and effective central institutions exist. Certainly, the task involved, to form a common European economy, is sufficiently interesting to arouse significant national, social, and economic forces within the member countries. But are the tasks of economic integration inherently expansive and, if so, will their expansiveness lead to a European government? The answer is believed to be tied to the fourth condition: will the member states continue to see their interests as consistent with the whole supranational enterprise?

For those involved with the Common Market, it seems an article of faith that the economic functions it performs are expansive, that a European federal government is only a logical development of the forces already set to work, and finally that the process has already gone so far as to be nearly irreversible by any member state.

As tariff barriers fall, the official argument runs, competition is increasingly between separate firms rather than whole national economies, and it becomes more and more essential that the conditions of competition be roughly the same throughout the whole market.[33] Otherwise some individual firms are given special advantages. Where taxes, wages, laws and regulations, energy prices, or transportation costs are markedly different, those areas which impose unfavorable conditions will inevitably suffer. The natural tendency, then, is towards as much uniformity as possible.

Hence economic integration is expected to impose a great check on the freedom of action of the national governments. General laws and regulations that affect business will have to be harmonized, and wages, social security, and welfare costs equalized. The costs of raw materials cannot be allowed to differ markedly and so there must be a common external tariff. Taxes, or even the method of taxation, cannot vary too much without affecting competition, and therefore a limit is placed upon the ability of one government to follow unique policies that are extremely expensive. There might seem to be a limit, for example, on how much a government could spend on defense without cutting its other expenditures. A common economy would seem to imply a common trade or commercial policy towards the outside world. And it seems only reasonable, as in the recent trade talks between the EEC and the United States, that the negotiations should be conducted by the Commission acting for the whole Community rather than by each member state separately.[34] Since foreign policy is closely related to trade, economic integration can be expected to press towards a single foreign policy as well.

In a world where economic planning is commonplace, it is argued, progressive economic integration will lead to strong pressure for positive policies from a source that plans for the whole European economy. Fiscal policies will have to be in general harmony. It will not be reasonable to have a deflationary policy in one area and an inflationary one in another. As planning centers more and more around the supranational Community, its decisions will naturally have an increasing effect on the daily lives of the people of Europe.[35] As present, the Community institutions are notable in that they appear so remote from popular control. In the democratic West, it is unacceptable that power should not be responsible to elected representatives of the people. Therefore, a popularly elected political body, a genuine European Parliament, can be expected to follow inevitably. Thus, according to the official ideology, the inexorable logic of economic integration is moving Europe slowly towards political union.

4.

The Common Market argument is powerful and seductive. Does it accord with the facts? What are the real prospects for political unity to develop from economic integration alone? While the degree to which economic integration inhibits independent governmental policies may be exaggerated, there is no question but that continuing economic fusion calls for at least some increase in political unity. But will economic integration necessarily continue advancing? Can it be stopped or reversed?

At the present time, it is the national governments which hold the keys to the future. The progress of the Common Market depends upon their policies in the Council. It is almost axiomatic that the process of economic integration will continue as long as the member governments find its advance in their interest. It may also be true that the true economic interests of all Europe lie with economic and political union. But the crude Marxist premise that economic considerations determine political events is blatantly untrue.

Nations, communist nations above all, are constantly undertaking policies which are economically harmful if not ruinous in pursuit of goals which seem more important to them than the extra margin of economic well-being. Nations have been known to go to war and assume untold economic damage for the sake of honor, pride, grandeur, power, or faith. Economic growth does indeed have a logic of development, an idea of its own, but then so does nationalism. And time and time again in the past two centuries, the dynamics of nationalism have triumphed over the apparent logic of economics.

But although economic factors may not determine everything, they certainly pose a certain limit beyond which national policy cannot go without being self-destructive. The great question is whether a national government of the Six could now afford to pull out. Has it already become too costly to withdraw? When will the dynamic process have advanced so far that the Common Market can assume the continuing commitment of the national states?

At the present stage of unity, it is generally felt that a national government could withdraw, although the economic repercussions would be severe and therefore not lightly assumed by any popularly elected government in an opulent Western society.[36] There are knowledgeable government officials who argue, at least privately, that the costs of withdrawing have been greatly exaggerated. They argue that although the increase in trade among the Six has been enormous, it is by no means clear that the increase which has taken place within the Common Market has taken place because of it.[37] Some economists have maintained that the rapid increase of trade among developed countries is a universal phenomenon and would have happened in Europe with or without the Common Market.[38] Furthermore, the whole general tendency towards an Atlantic market embodied in the Kennedy Round may change the particular relationship of the Six.[39] Hence a state might withdraw without necessarily suffering a drastic cut, even in its European trade. And while formidable tariff barriers, should they exist, might close off foreign markets, they could also eliminate foreign competitors in the domestic market.

It is significant, however, that the big businessmen who weigh these gains and losses in their own affairs, are among the most vociferous supporters of the Common Market. Their support is a great source of comfort to the Communities. Especially enthusiastic are those giant industries which are too developed for their own national markets—such as Belgian steel or Dutch agriculture. But efficient or at least imaginative business everywhere seems to welcome the Continental market. French industrialists, once fearful and protectionist, are now among the strongest supporters of the EEC. Furthermore, with their strong national predilection for planning, they are among the most insistent advocates of more central power to assure the safeguards, control, and harmonization they believe necessary to make the European economy realize efficiently its potential.[40] Hence, the Common Market can claim that there has been a fundamental change in the perspectives and habits of European businessmen. Business in Europe is committed to integration and it would be extremely difficult for a national government to reverse that commitment.

Skeptics argue that big business has always been internationalist. There have always been agreements and personal contact among European businessmen. The conditions for carrying on international business in Europe still have a long way to go before they reach the ease that was commonplace before the First World War. Even Hallstein admits that the Common Market is hoping to restore that freedom of trade which existed before war and economic crises caused "the old pattern of world trade" to disappear.[41] And while there have been numerous agreements among similar industries, skeptics continue, there has in fact been remarkably little supranational merging among the Six themselves. Figures showing the relative degree of investment of the Six in each other are hard to come by, but some seasoned observers claim that as yet it is surprisingly slight. National firms have tended either to remain national or to merge with giant American companies. It seems as if American capital, and not the Common Market, will be the federalizer of European business. The tendency of European firms to go to the United States for capital is widely deplored, but as yet there is nothing like an adequate capital market within the Six.[42]

Another factor cited by those who seek to minimize the permanence of integration is the supposed tendency of each national economy to move towards greater autarchy rather than towards a genuine Continental rationalization. Each nation, it is argued, instead of concentrating further on what it does best, has tended to develop its own full range of manufactures and thus in fact reduce its eventual dependence on its neighbors. Italy, for example, has developed a steel industry.

No doubt there is a good deal to some of these skeptical arguments. European economic integration must travel a long way before it is possible to speak of an indivisible Continental economy from which no sane government would possibly withdraw. But certainly important progress towards integration has been made. And however inconclusive previous moves may have been, the agricultural agreements of 1962 and 1964 are unquestionably a major if not irrevocable step. Ironically, it is the country ostensibly the most concerned with guarding its national independence, France, which would appear to be the most committed by the new agreements.

The net result of a common market in agriculture is that the French have succeeded in throwing the burden of their surplus on the rest of Europe. These arrangements are hardly natural. The Germans could buy food more cheaply outside Europe and by doing so help win markets for their manufactures. The French, through the politics of European integration, have solved a serious domestic situation. Any French government that renounced these new advantages would be taking grave political risks at home. On the other hand, the common market in agriculture would seem to imply or even to require further integration which cannot help but limit the political independence so cherished by Gaullist France.

The agricultural common market, because it requires so much conscious contrivance, illustrates to a heightened degree the dynamic tendency of economic integration to expand from one field to the next and to pass over into politics. To have a common market in agriculture, it is essential to have a common central regulatory organization which, among other things, sets common support prices for every commodity. The artificially controlled prices must be roughly the same throughout the Six. Since prices are expressed in terms of national currency, it is now argued that no European country can devalue its currency without raising its food prices. Otherwise food prices in one country would be lower than in the others, dumping would result, and the whole system would be deranged. On the other hand, if the devaluing country raised its domestic food prices, it would seriously undermine the effects of devaluation. The net result, the argument runs, is that it is no longer possible for one of the Six to devalue, not at any rate without destroying the Common Market, at least in agriculture.[43] Since devaluation is generally seen as the ultimate weapon of a government which is following policies which make its industries noncompetitive—too high taxes for the soaring costs of a nuclear deterrent, for example—it is felt that the agricultural agreements in the Common Market will impose a strong monetary and fiscal discipline on all states and point towards a common fiscal policy.

Not only, however, does the supranational solution to France's agricultural problem lead to important new curbs on national independence, but it results in a major increase in power to the Community itself. It is the Commission which is to administer the complex program with the huge sums necessary to finance it. Not content with this substantial accretion of power to the Community, the Commission seized the occasion to propose that all tariff revenues should go to the Community and that the European Parliament should have a voice in the disposition of the huge sums that would be involved.[44] Furthermore, the Commission has argued that since the Community pays to support Europe's farmers, it should have a veto over any export sales below the support price. Such power would be an important step towards a common commercial policy towards the outside world, and would, in turn, seriously impinge on national control over trade agreements, an important weapon of peaceful diplomacy. In short, there seem to be few limits to this imaginative train of logical extensions following from agricultural integration.

In summary, the technical arguments over how much integration has occurred are so complex and debatable that they seem beyond the power of laymen to understand or professionals to agree upon. There does appear, nevertheless, to be a logic to economic development which leads even the most recalcitrant governments into limitations on their independence from which they probably cannot escape without pulling out of the Common Market—a costly step. The Six could break up, but even if they continue to compose their differences, does that mean that the spill-over process of economic and political integration will necessarily go on until Europe has a federal government? Not necessarily.[45]

To achieve a certain degree of integration is one thing, to go on with it is another. There is no mindless inevitable law of economics which compels the transition. States are free agents in the same sense that any conscious being is free. They are hedged in by circumstances, but they have a number of choices before them. If they cannot afford the increased independence that would come from pulling out of the Common Market, there is nothing which compels them to sacrifice further independence for further economic gains. Moreover, even assuming that integration does prevent governments from raising taxes beyond the general level, that may not be in itself a serious handicap to independence. Proponents of General de Gaulle's *force de frappe*, for example, argue that it costs less than an old-fashioned army. France, while building an atomic force, formally reduced her military budget by a great deal. An expanding economy offers any government the opportunity to increase substantially its expenditures in any one field without either raising taxes or cutting back in other fields.[46] It can be argued perversely that the Common Market, by strengthening the economies of the members, has increased their means of political independence.

Even if it is true that more and more national decisions will have to be referred to the Community at Brussels, it would be unrealistic to equate growth in the importance of Community decisions with an increase of supranational at the expense of national power. The Community, after all, means the Council as well as the Commission. The success of the Community institutions has always depended upon the active political will of the member states. If the political will to integrate the European economy disappeared, the "miracle" in Brussels might continue, but would not progress. The death of Europe would not necessarily be dramatic. Problems would simply be left to the experts and hence remain unsolved.

While the national veto is supposed to be replaced in 1966 by a qualified system of majority voting, any change is likely to be only a formality. Almost any one of the Six, and certainly any of the major powers, will still be able to slow down the whole process of integration, stop it altogether, or even set it back. A state can follow an "empty-chair policy, for example, and absent itself from the Council and various working committees.[47] Since the whole spirit of the Council is necessarily cooperative rather than coercive, the threat of such a policy might well be enough in itself to constitute a *de facto* veto.

Furthermore, the much vaunted independence of the Commission and its admittedly indispensable role as catalyst for common policies depends finally on the indulgence of the national governments. Most of the members of the Commission and its staff are national civil servants on leave from their national governments. The French, in particular, have encouraged many of their finest civil servants to take posts in the Common Market administration.[48] By taking severe retaliation on those functionaries who showed independence, or simply by not appointing men of ability and political initiative in the first place, it would be quite possible to reduce the quality of the European civil service and hence the now admirable effectiveness of the whole organization. Once the Common Market Commission really was made up of technicians without the extraordinary political skills of the present members, the whole push towards integration would slacken. It is said that the Coal and Steel Community has suffered from just such a decline.

In short the Common Market, for all the imaginative diplomatic skill of its executive and for all the administrative responsibility it has gradually gathered to itself, is still mainly dependent on the political will of the member states. Though there is clearly a logic of integration which, if allowed free rein, tends to accelerate the federalizing process towards political unification, it is doubtful if there is any inherent force in the process itself which compels the national states to follow along to the inherent conclusion.

Unless the states will otherwise, the Common Market can easily become not a federal government for Europe, but a sort of apolitical regulatory body, with real powers of its own, to be sure, but always subject ultimately to the political control of the states. The Common Market could thus become, not the nascent government of Europe, but a bureaucratic business manager for the economies of the Continent. It would remain an institutionalized monument to a dream from the past; it would survive only because it had found a way to be useful to its masters. The supranational community would become a sort of secular church, a church whose priests were rich and powerful but in whose religion no one really believed anymore.

In short, it is difficult to accept the thesis that the success of the Common Market as a federal government is assured by an inherent, autonomous logic of economic integration. If the Common Market is to unify Europe, it must expect to change the course of history, not float along placidly on the existing current of events. While spill-over may be useful as an ideology to warm the faithful, it would seem to offer in itself a meager basis for expecting a federal Europe to grow inevitably out of the Common Market.

It may be sad to realize that no impersonal economic law guarantees their success, but fortunately the supranational Communities enjoy other sources of power than the logic of economic integration. It is somewhat unreal to study European unity as if it owed its strength to a "process" rather than an idea. For there can be few movements which illustrate better the force of ideas or which depend more upon that force. Indeed, it is probably true that the major impulse behind European unity is less economic than psychological and political.[49] According to the President of the Commission itself: "The reasons why European unity is useful, necessary, inevitable, are quickly enumerated. They are mainly psychological. . . ."[50] The exhilarating sense of spaciousness, liberation, and renewed power that surrounds the dream of a united Europe may be more likely to create that Europe than calculations about the advantages of large-scale marketing.

Those calculations are, in any case, usually themselves part of the larger dream. In particular, the prospect of Europe's reviving into a great power is a strong force behind the European communities. A few minutes' conversation with an ardent partisan of supranational Europe usually provides ample evidence that his nationalism has not so much died as shifted to the new nation the Communities are believed to be creating. In Hallstein's words:

> We are trying to replace one political prejudice that has for centuries past swayed human beings in Europe, that has made the political map of Europe what it is today—the national prejudice—by a better attitude, a European attitude—provided you do not take it as a piece of cynicism, I would even say: by a better, a European, prejudice.[51]

That European force should not be underestimated, no matter how inadequate the theories or institutions with which it momentarily seeks to express itself. The Common Market has attracted such extraordinary ardor and ability that it would be premature to write off the men of Brussels along with the theories of their partisans.

Whatever the power of the new European loyalties, the individual nations are far from dead. It may well be that nationalism is discredited among Italians and above all Germans who, for understandable reasons, are desperately seeking for a new political identity. But not everyone is as eager to escape from his national past. In France, after all, nationalism produced not Hitler but de Gaulle. The French Resistance, unlike the Italian, was intensely nationalistic. In contrast to Altiero Spinelli, the chief theorist of the French was Michel Debré.[52]

And while a few years ago it used to be taken for granted that we were in "an era of concentration," today there is some reason to think that the impulse to unify may have depended on economic and political pressures that are to some extent subsiding.[53] Doubtless sentiment for unity is still very strong among Europeans. But it is hardly so strong that unity can be treated as a foregone conclusion, dictated by inexorable automatic processes. For the real power of the national states remains virtually untouched. It is they alone who command the organized political loyalties of their peoples. Even in the citadel of supranational Europe, it is the states who hold the determining power.

Under the circumstances, it would not seem unreasonable to predict that the drive for a federal Europe will take its decisive step only when the supranational institutions find some way to escape from their complete dependence on the cooperation of the national governments. In a democratic world where legitimacy comes from the people, supranational Europe must ultimately find the means for a direct, organized, political relationship with the peoples it hopes to govern. Otherwise, it will never be able to challenge the national governments in the ultimately decisive arena, that is, before their own people. Until then the functionaries of Brussels may prove to be what some nationalists call them—flies of the summer, likely to be blown away by the first big storm.

5.

Conclusions about the essential political weakness of the Common Market are no doubt more strongly stated here than in most writing on the subject. But they are views which are held widely, above all by many European federalists outside the Common Market. The official line of the Common Market Commission is a good deal more optimistic. The Eurocrats are a special breed, different from other federalists. They have their own view of the world, of a new society, which can be gleaned not only from their conversation but from their own official statements. The writings of the Commission's President, Walter Hallstein, are especially revealing. Though it would appear that the present institutions of the Community leave it absolutely dependent on the good will of the national states, he appears to find these institutions essentially satisfactory. The present Communities are called economic, but they are already political. They are not "preparation" for political union: "No they are the centre piece, the finished section of an edifice which when completed will be the political federation of Europe." [54] "Experience thus lends no support to the view that our constitution for Europe already needs to be amended if the Community is to be fully realized." [55]

In the President's view, in short, the present structure is admirable. It prevents big-power domination, yet leadership for the over-all good of Europe is provided through the energetic initiative and mediation of the independent Commission.[56] Meanwhile, the critical economic elites are increasingly directing their attention towards Brussels and being drawn into a European rather than a national focus.[57] It would nevertheless be desirable, the President concludes, to have direct democratic elections to the European Parliament.[58] In any event, that body ought to be given a greater role in legislation—not to change the decisions that have been taken all along by the Council, but to dramatize them for public opinion:

> The real problem is rather that, as it has no substantive power of decision, the Parliament's role of dramatizing and popularizing the great decisions—which is what makes it a decisive factor in forming public opinion—cannot be played with full effect. The danger is not that the Community's progress will be halted by this, but that the Community may become too remote to be understood.[59]

The President's statements reflect a number of characteristic ideas and attitudes and, indeed, offer a glimpse into that whole view of politics which informs the grand alternative posed by the functionalists of Brussels. To begin with, there is a marked if not surprising faith in the wisdom and virtue of bureaucratic experts. The record of the Eurocrats is impressive, but the uncommitted observer is still led to ask some skeptical questions. It is asserted continually, for example, that the Commission always represents the general interest of the Community in contrast to the national states who assert particular interests.[60] But the nature of the general interest is not always easy to resolve. In large political questions, why should cosmopolitan bureaucrats be more farseeing than national politicians? The Commission, moreover, sees itself as the guardian of the small states against the big.[61] But why are the interests of small states somehow more compatible with the general interest of Europe? Considering its power and place in the world, it may be that the great states know better how to play Europe's role than the small. The Commission, which is remarkably free from direct democratic control, is accumulating more and more formidable administrative power. What will keep that power from corrupting Commissioners as it has so frequently corrupted the executives of other political systems?

Closely allied to Hallstein's faith in the wisdom and virtue of experts is his apparent faith in their ability to resolve conflicts.[62] But what reason is there to assume that all economic and social conflicts can be resolved without bitter struggle? National states still have to deal with bitterly divisive issues—even in this time of advancing prosperity. Why should these issues not exist within the far greater disparities of a European economy? [63] And again the old problem: what happens if a national state refuses to cooperate? In a conflict between the Community and a national state, who holds the real power? Eventually Hallstein expects the Community to develop a greater and greater network of supporters among the elites who control public opinion. But who can focus that loyalty? Who can go over the heads of national governments and appeal directly to the people? Who can speak in the name of Europe in a voice that is recognized as the people's choice?

The democratic political dimension of the Communities was intended to come from the European Parliament. President Hallstein, in common with nearly all partisans of supranational Europe, makes the strengthening of that Parliament a primary goal of his political policy. At the moment, the Parliament is the weakest organ of the Communities.[64] Its members are chosen by the national parliaments from among those deputies who are enthusiastic enough about Europe to take the time to attend the sessions. Hence it is mainly composed of good Europeans who support the Commission on principle because it is supranational as opposed to the nationalist Council of Ministers. The Parliament can and does debate issues, but, perversely, dismissing the Commission is its only real power. In short, its only control applies to the very group it wants more than any other to support.

To strengthen the Parliament, the Commission presented its ingenious proposal to give that body a major voice in distributing the vast surplus revenues which agriculture and trade integration were expected to bring to the Community.[65] Numerous consequences might have been predicted. Once the Parliament had such great power, there would of course be a more compelling incentive towards the truly significant step of choosing its members by direct elections.[66] Direct elections would give the Parliament democratic legitimacy and hence the Community would be greatly strengthened in relation to the national states. The power of a democratic assembly would inevitably grow and the balance of preponderance would shift to it. The Council might eventually be reduced to a second chamber made up of diplomatic representatives from the member states, like the present German *Bundesrat*. The Parliament might be expected to gain the right to elect the Commission and thus the Common Market would acquire a responsible executive. Europe would then have, for all intents and purposes, a federal government.

It is a beguiling vision of the future but the road to it, direct elections, is a course as full of possible peril as it is of profit. Even partisans of the Community have serious misgivings. To begin with, there is the danger that since the Parliament still has little power, no one will be interested in voting and the whole election will result in a general loss of prestige for the Communities. The plan to give it power over the budget is, of course, designed to counter this argument. Secondly, however, it can be argued that the influence of the Parliament is greater because its members belong to a national body where they can present the Community's point of view and bring pressure to bear on their own governments. But the really serious danger would most likely come from the changes direct elections would make in the Parliament itself.

A genuinely "politicized" Parliament would very likely be a far greater hindrance to the effectiveness of the Commission than a check on the Council. At the moment, the Commission's independence has almost no interference from any source. Hence it enjoys great freedom of action in drawing up proposals. It is not continually forced to defend itself; it does not have to defer constantly to public opinion; it can operate with great discretion—thus much of its diplomatic success in harmonizing the clashes of interest among the member states. Anything which interfered with its independence might well hamstring its work and greatly decrease its effectiveness. An elected Parliament would probably bring about just such interference. A democratic

European Parliament could be expected to reflect a much fuller range of popular opinion which is hardly unanimous on the necessity, let alone the method, of remaking Europe. It would be composed of deputies concerned with winning elections—hence the work of the Common Market would become the focus of partisan multinational debates among parties bidding for interest votes. It is hard to imagine an arrangement more likely to disrupt the development of the Communities than making the Commission responsible to such a Parliament.

President Hallstein professes to see none of these dangers. He does not anticipate that a democratic Parliament would have any great effect on the content of the decisions taken by the Common Market. For him, Parliament's role is "dramatizing and popularizing the great decisions." Popular government is chiefly a technique of public relations.

It cannot be said that such a view of parliaments is unique nowadays. It is shared by nearly all those who believe that strong executive government has become a necessity in the modern world. Parliaments have, in fact, generally declined. While the increasing complexity of affairs has given immense new powers to government, that very complexity has proved the downfall of the legislature. Such large bodies often appear too cumbersome and indecisive to direct affairs—to resolve the issues and control bureaucrats. In many countries the political function has shifted from parliaments to presidents and prime ministers. Strong men, using the power of mass communication to draw strength from the people, have taken over the tasks of rule. It is one of the paradoxes of modern politics that a kind of elected monarchy seems the typical form of government for a large-scale democracy. It is the president who represents the people and parliament the elite. While that may have been the deplorable pattern of Napoleon III and Mussolini, it is also true of government in the United States and even in parliamentary Britain.

There has been some speculation in Brussels about the possibility of a democratic President of Europe. The difficulties of finding the man and the machinery are discouraging enough, but there is no real interest. Significantly, Michel Debré, de Gaulle's first Prime Minister, seems almost the only theorist who ever seriously considered building European unity around a presidential system.[67] But in Brussels, no one has, and apparently no one wants, the terrible power to do what de Gaulle or Johnson can do—appear on television and, as the embodiment of the nation, summon directly the loyalties of millions of countrymen.

The whole notion of a democratic politician as master seems foreign to the atmosphere of the European Communities. Assuredly the Eurocrats are politicans, as they rightfully claim to be. But their politics are the politics of administration, of bureaucratic elites, and not of mass democracy. It seems as if their attempt to turn the institutions of the EEC into the future government of Europe is powered not only by the drive to build Europe, but by the desire to propose a substitute for that form of presidential government which has come increasingly to predominate within the modern national state. The Eurocrats are unlike many of the federalist theorists, one suspects, because they are less interested in the revival of parliaments than in developing a new form of executive government.

Parliament for Hallstein, as for Debré, exists not to make decisions but to publicize them. But whereas Debré would replace the democratic political function of Parliament with a democratic king, it almost seems as if the Eurocrats want that function to disappear altogether. The relation between the European Parliament and the Commission is compared to that between stockholders and directors.[68] The analogy is revealing. Political leadership is a question of professional management efficiency. As long as the dividends keep coming, the public is satisfied. When the dividends fall, the old *equipe* is sacked and a new set of professional managers take over.

To the unsympathetic, the theories of the men of Brussels are only the rationalization of vigorous bureaucrats seeking to preserve and expand their powers. Their new Europe would be an idealized Austro-Hungarian Empire without Franz-Josef. Their dreams are those of functionaries throughout the ages—a royal bureaucracy without the king. The Europe they would build is the "Europe of the Mandarins."

But behind the extraordinary energy and elan of Brussels is something more than vigorous bureaucratic empire-building. While the Eurocrats are less philosophers than men of action, there is an ideal that is strong among them. It might be called the technocratic ideal.[69] It is a dream of what government could be in a world where, in Hallstein's words: "Man's intellectual mastery not only of nature but also of social—including economic—processes has in our time grown as never before."[70] That ideal, though seldom spelled out in a formal system, represents today perhaps the most formidable of all the challenges to nationalist views on the state.

The basic tenet of this technocratic philosophy is that many of the problems that presently plague humankind could be solved if only decisions could be left to impartial, scientifically trained experts whose efforts were not continually distorted by the emotional and hasty generalizations of mass politics. The roots of this faith in experts are to be found in the Englightenment dream of a world governed by reason instead of vulgar prejudice. The dream inspired the Positivist movement of the nineteenth century—Bentham in England and St. Simon and Comte in France.

It has gained increasing credence as the prestige of physical science has soared, as economics and even industry have taken on more and more the trappings of a mathematical science, and as so many economic and political decisions have come to rely on information processed by experts and their computers. It is essentially the philosophy of the *haut fonctionnaire* of government and business, many of whom were impressed during the war with how easily international difficulties might quietly be settled among high civil servants.[71] Such awareness might be expected to be particularly strong among the great bureaucrats of the European Communities who have so often found rational solutions that avoided popularized political conflict. They could do much more, they believe, if only given the chance. In the modern world, conflict is often needless.

It is generally the vulgarization of political decision-making by popular emotions, prejudices, and slogans that has prevented the full harvest of man's new skill in controlling his environment. Nationalism is to be feared precisely because its essence lies in the ceaseless emotional participation of the populace in the affairs of government. The form of nationalism most to be feared is that which endows a single magnified leader with the whole of the awesome and fickle power of the people. In such a system, all the immense new force mobilized by modern technology becomes subject to direction by the vagaries of personality and megalomania.

Both the technocrat and the federalist dislike nationalism. Whereas the federalist finds nationalism undesirable, the technocrat believes it unnecessary. In the nineteenth century, it is argued, man's imperfect economic development and control led inevitably to politics dominated by the fear of scarcity. Competition was the law of life because there was not, in fact, enough to go around. But as Western economics have progressed to the "take-off point" and beyond, distribution and not scarcity has become the problem. There is no fundamental economic cause for social disharmony in the contemporary Western world. Therefore, politics is no longer the desperate class struggle it was a century ago. The problem of consensus is greatly eased. All the tremendous paraphernalia of nationalism—the continual cultivation of national loyalty through democratic participation—once essential to head off open class war, is now obsolete. The mass participation demanded by nationalism now merely interferes with the rational ordering of complex economic affairs.

For the votaries of the technocratic ideal, the mass politics of nationalism are obsolete not only as a practical method of government, but as a form of secular religion. With the decline of

Christianity, it is argued, politics tended for a time to become a substitute for religion. The sentiment perhaps still survived in the Personalists. To be a person, it was necessary to be a voter. Manhood required suffrage. But in today's world, the naive expectation of the ennobling results of political participation has been discredited. Nationalism has implicated the people in dreadful excesses. Popular politics have ennobled neither politics nor the people. Political apathy has become the sensible reaction of the average citizen, at least as long as a skillful government can maintain peace and full employment. The average man will be content to enjoy the new opulence technology will bring him. Even if there are no more grand adventures, there will be plenty of comfort.

In summary, the technocratic ideal attacks the very foundation of nationalist theory because it argues that consensus is no longer so difficult to obtain that it requires an intense cultivation of unity within a limited exclusive context. Thus it is that the technocrat joins the federalists in dislike for the "personalization of power" in the hands of today's version of monarchy—the presidential leader. Both federalist and functionalist prefer parliamentary government, government by committee, the rule by compromise and bargaining which allows no one element to dominate and creates no political power which can truly control the bureaucracy.

It is fascinating to speculate on the gathering conflict between today's monarch and his technocratic councilors. Both, in their fashion, are products of the discouraging complexity of modern affairs. Their struggle represents in modern dress the most recent episode in the age-old conflict between monarchy and aristocracy, or, in other words, between the rule that appeals to the many and that which appeals to the best. No doubt the future, like the past, will see the uneasy coexistence of both. Perhaps it will be the mandarins rather than the parliament which will be the real balance to the new monarchy.[72] Modern political communities cannot do without the technocrat; neither, probably, can they do without the chief.

They cannot, at least, if they are interested in power. The Eurocrats of Brussels are not bashful about wanting and needing power to build their new Europe. Hallstein is no passive federalist, happy to relax in the small comforts of local government. He believes:

> We live in a time of revolutionary change, which is divined by the arts and which is leading science to a new conception of the world. We cannot make ourselves masters of these times with political methods and procedures geared to the concepts of the past. Time must be taken by the forelock—and this applies in particular to politics, above all to European politics.[73]

Yet the power to take time by the forelock is unlikely to flow from bureaucracy alone. Someone must summon the people against the recalcitrant interests of the past.

Nor are the Eurocrats interested in a Europe which plays no powerful role in the world at large. For Hallstein, the Atlantic Alliance means equal partnership:

> Partnership means the opposite of a monolithic Atlantic Community in which the European states would play the part of a bridgehead towards the East, as were the Hellenic settlements in Asia Minor . . . Free Europe must develop its own personality in order to become a partner for America and to serve as a magnet for the countries of Eastern Europe.[74]

But it is likely that Europe as an equal partner to America will need a chief who can act with an authority equal to his American counterpart. The presidential system gives too strong an advantage to the state that has it over the state that does not. Any new Europe will be potentially a very great power. It is not likely to remain content either with the style or the role of a gargantuan Switzerland. Sooner or later, if there is to be a Europe it will need a king.

IV.

De Gaulle's Nationalist Europe

IV.

De Gaulle's
Nationalist
Europe

1.

Charles de Gaulle is almost the only major Western political leader who is an outspoken nationalist.[1] But he seems sufficiently formidable to freeze the movement towards European federal unity and, if he lives long enough, to wreck it. How is it possible for one man to thwart the hopes of so many good Europeans?

In studying de Gaulle, it is all too easy to become preoccupied with his singular personality and style, and as a result, to overlook what has made him genuinely important: in the famous quarrels of his lifetime, he has often been right and his opponents wrong. Pétain had grandeur even in ruin, but he was wrong—both about the nature of modern war and about the best course for defeated France. Roosevelt was a fascinating personality and a superb political manipulator, but he knew much less than de Gaulle about the political realities of Europe. The Fourth Republic had a number of able leaders with imaginative programs, but it was de Gaulle who at last gave France a government capable of making and holding to decisions. In short, de Gaulle, while often accused of being out of step with his times, has again and again confounded his critics because he has seen more clearly than they the political and strategic realities of the modern world. Ultimately, it is his vision that has given him power over events, not his personality. Today if his nationalist ideas seem curiously anachronistic, it still behooves the wise observer to study them carefully.

What is de Gaulle's vision of Europe? He has been unyieldingly hostile to the supranational pretensions of the Common Market, but he has energetically encouraged European economic integration. His supporters would claim in addition that he has proposed the only realistic scheme for European political unity. His approach is confederal rather than supranational. He would build Europe around the existing national states rather than a new federal center. De Gaulle's union would seek to coordinate national policies wherever possible while leaving the political sovereignty of the states intact.

De Gaulle's present European views date from the war. While his prewar writings show a keen sense of Europe as a community of interdependent states, his notions of how to organize that interdependence never strayed beyond traditional theories of the balance of power.[2] His views developed rapidly in the war.[3] He

seemed convinced that close alliances were an ineluctable consequence of the general evolution of affairs.[4] In 1944 he remarked in
a press conference: "I believe that we are in an age of concentration."[5] His troubles with the Anglo-Saxon allies led him to
dream of an alliance of his own, a European coalition led by
France—"a sort of Western grouping" which, without infringing
on the sovereignty of anyone, would constitute a major world
center for production, trade, and security. Its "arteries" would be
the Channel, the Rhine, and the Mediterranean, but it would be
"extended" through Africa and the Orient.[6]

Any such continental grouping would necessarily be based, de
Gaulle believed, upon a fundamental agreement between France
and Germany. In spite of their sins, the Germans were a great
people whose destruction was proscribed by "the higher logic of
Europe." De Gaulle visited Germany in May, 1945. While observing the smoking ruins and musing over the fate of the territories
occupied by the Russians, he notes: "I felt my sense of distrust
and severity fade within me. I even glimpsed possibilities of
understanding which the past had never offered; moreover, it
seemed to me that the same sentiment was dawning among
our soldiers."[7]

De Gaulle's own solution to the German problem, however, was
severe enough: to break up the Reich and put its pieces into a
general European confederation. Before Prussia coerced them
into unity there had been many German states; there should be
again. The new states could find their place within a general
European confederation.[8]

The *Memoirs* speak as if de Gaulle had launched an extensive
campaign for European unity in 1946, near the end of his tenure
as President of the Provisional Government. Indeed, the *Memoirs*
imply that his enthusiasm for Europe was yet another issue
separating him from the French parties.[9] But de Gaulle's public
speeches on European unity in this period seem more restrained
than the *Memoirs* suggest. In any event, he was soon to lose

control of his country. Like Churchill, de Gaulle defeated seemed to be a good European. Both leaders proposed roughly the same confederal scheme. Each may well have expected his own country to be the leader.

When in 1947 de Gaulle launched his new political party, the *Rassemblement du Peuple Français*, the European theme was a major element in its platform. In a series of speeches and press conferences, he elaborated his confederal scheme for "Europe made up of free men and independent states, organized into a whole capable of containing all possible pretension to hegemony and establishing between the two rival masses the element of equilibrium without which peace will never come about." [10]

The Council of Europe, established in 1949, might have seemed the first step towards establishing the confederal Europe de Gaulle was seeking. But for the Gaullists, the Council was a false start. They admitted that it had noted and even illustrious men associated with it. "But how," they asked, "can we be made to believe that this institution, which has no European mandate, no effective power, no real responsibility, is going to forge the colossal work of the union of a continent?" [11] The Council was a British creation and, as such, mirrored faithfully Britain's lack of real interest in European unity. As an alternative, de Gaulle proposed an early version of the Fouchet Plan. The building of Europe should be launched, he argued, by a giant referendum asking the people to give a clear expression of their will towards unity. A constitutional assembly, thus fortified by popular support, should elaborate the institutions of the European Confederacy which would be the first step towards union. The Confederacy would conjugate the policies of the states, especially in the fields of economics, defense, and culture. [12]

De Gaulle had reconciled himself to a West German Federal Government and found the prospects for a Franco-German entente promising. [13] If Western Europe could be securely forged around a Franco-German entente, de Gaulle continued grandly, Europe with its African extension and with the support of the

United States could turn to Russia: "It will be possible to try, once and for all, to make a whole Europe with Russia included, she having been obliged to change her regime. That is the program of true Europeans. That is mine." [14]

It was not to be the program of most other people who considered themselves true Europeans. The federalists especially, while they came to share de Gaulle's views on the Council of Europe, saw little to be gained from his form of confederation. To them de Gaulle's plans, in text and above all in spirit, were nothing but old-fashioned nationalism, even if of a rather imaginative variety. Progress towards a united Europe depended, they believed, not upon close cooperation between the old nations—a formula that had failed many times—but upon building new supranational institutions that would gradually eliminate the old nationalist states. Their hopes for union led along the path of the Coal and Steel Community, the European Army, Euratom, and the Common Market. For de Gaulle, that was a route which led to disenchantment and danger.

2.

The quarrel between de Gaulle and the partisans of supranational Europe is centered around the question of what it takes to build a political community capable of playing an active role in the outside world. In de Gaulle's view, nothing but a state can play such a role and none of the various supranational communities has possessed or ever had the capability to possess the characteristics essential to a state. To have an effective state, de Gaulle believes it is necessary to have a "political, economic, financial, administrative, and, above all, moral entity sufficiently living, established and recognized to obtain the congenital loyalty of its subjects, to have a political policy of its own, and, if it should happen, that millions of men would be willing to die for it." [15] Supranational bodies are not states but "alchemic mixtures, algebraic combinations and cabalistic formulas." [16]

De Gaulle's criticisms have centered around three main points. To begin with, none of the existing or proposed institutions has had, in his view, any real political foundation. The often attractive, able, and even illustrious men are all essentially technocrats rather than politicians. Thus although they have their technical value, they have no real authority over the peoples of Europe and, in moments of crisis, it is only the states that can act. [17]

To have political power, it is necessary to have institutions which are seen to flow from the popular will and thus engage the loyal support of the people. Without such power, no government can lead its people through the trials which history imposes. Not only are the supranational Communities without the political roots which they would need to rule, but they are by their very nature incapable of forming and carrying out a coherent general policy for the society they are meant to govern. That is, at any rate, the second major Gaullist criticism of the Communities—they would fragment the power of the state until a coherent public policy would become impossible. Every one of the Communities has been based on the assumption that it is possible to deal separately with particular aspects of European life—the army, the coal and steel industry, or atomic power. De Gaulle rejects this whole approach, so dear to functionalists and personalists alike. He opposed the Coal and Steel Community, for example, on the grounds that it was ridiculous to isolate one section of the economy for supranational control while leaving all the rest still subject to national governments. It is perhaps significant that he has seemed more favorable to the Common Market which takes into consideration the whole of Europe's economic life. [18]

While the Communities, with their unreal power and fragmented competence, could never be an effective government for Europe, they could succeed in robbing the old national states of their faculties and thus there would be no institutions left in Europe capable of performing the role of a state.[19] That is the third major Gaullist criticism of the federalist Communities. If successful, they would leave Europe in a political vacuum which others with hegemonic predilections would be only too eager to fill. For de Gaulle, a federal Europe means an American Europe. The federalists, like the communists, work to undermine national governments in order to replace them by a foreign power.

De Gaulle has voiced roughly the same objection to all European Communities for the past fifteen years. His most vehement criticism was aroused by the most ambitious of all the federalist schemes, the European Defense Community. De Gaulle saw the European army, or rather "the army called European," as a peculiar military mélange, placed in the service of a vocable with no real existence called Europe.[20] Since Europe could not exist because it lacked a state to give it a political will, its so-called army would be a band of anational auxiliaries in the service, not of Europe which had no state, but of America. Probably the Europeans would even be under the command of an American general.[21] Militarily, as far as de Gaulle was concerned, such an arrangement would be lunatic: "I ask in the name of what can ardor, confidence and obedience be demanded from French citizens incorporated in an anational organism?" [22]

> At the base of the defense of peoples, there are the peoples themselves. This profound force cannot be replaced by technique. Wars are not fought simply by Pentagons, by GHQs, by Shapes, or NATOs. Wars are fought with the blood and souls of men. Neither European nor Atlantic defense can be built except on the base of realities and those realities are national. There are no others, except, of course, in the formularies of politicans.[23]

It was easy to see, de Gaulle continued, why England and America were interested in building such a European army. Their strategy for defending Europe was essentially peripheral. They were not willing to build up large land armies and commit them to the defense of the Continent. Since France could not have an army large enough to hold Russia alone, Germany had to be rearmed militarily—but it would be convenient if some formula could be found which kept Germany disarmed politically. The European army was the solution. What would happen, in effect, was that France would give up her independence in order to prevent Germany from gaining hers. It was instructive that the British would have nothing to do with the arrangments. It was the Americans who gained the most. How convenient for the Americans to have European allies who did what they were told and demanded so little in return. What a capital stroke of good fortune that these allies were willing to dissove their means of independent action and were actually asking to be commanded by America.

The Americans, de Gaulle continued, could hardly be blamed for taking advantage of the Europeans. Every nation, after all, was inclined to look out for its own interests first. A good ally demanded his rights in return. But the Europeans in particular, and France above all, seemed in the grip of a political "neurasthenia." They were eager to divest themselves of any means of independent action because fundamentally they hoped to renounce the responsibility for their own future. Thus they invited bullying by their powerful ally. They were willing to resign their military forces to American control without, in de Gaulle's opinion, even demanding in return adequate guarantees of protection against a Russian military invasion.[24]

With the defeat of the European army in 1954, de Gaulle withdrew from politics to write his *Memoirs*. On his return to power in 1958, he began again to press his old confederal scheme for a Europe of States while continuing to resist adamantly the political ambitions of the federalist Communities. While he grew to appreciate the services of the Eurocrats, he continued to argue that federation towards which they aspired would leave Europe without an effective state and hence too weak to resist the commands of its well-meaning but domineering American ally.[25]

A genuine state that embraced all Europe could not be created "without there being in Europe today a federator with sufficient power, authority and skill." There was no such federator:

> That is why one falls back on a type of hybrid, in which the six states would undertake to comply with what will be decided upon by a certain majority. . . .
>
> These are ideas that may, perhaps, beguile certain minds, but I certainly do not see how they could be carried out in practice, even if there were six signatures on the dotted line. Is there a France, a Germany, an Italy, a Holland, a Belgium, a Luxembourg, that would be ready—in a matter that is important for them from the national or the international point of view—to do something that they would consider bad because this would be dictated to them by others? Would the French people, the German people, the Italian people, the Dutch people, the Belgian people, or the Luxembourg people dream of submitting to laws voted by foreign deputies if these laws were to run contrary to their own deep-seated will? This is not so; there is no way, at the present time, for a foreign majority to be able to constrain recalcitrant nations.
>
> It is true that, in this "integrated" Europe, as they say, there would perhaps be no policy at all. This would simplify things a great deal. Indeed, once there would be no France and no Europe, once there would be no policy—since no one policy could be imposed on each of the six States—one would refrain from making any policies at all. But then, perhaps, this world would follow the lead of some outsider who did have a policy. There would perhaps be a federator, but the federator would not be European.[26]

De Gaulle used roughly the same argument in vetoing Britain's entry into the Common Market. The English, as he saw it, were not interested in building a Europe distinct from America. To begin with, England had few ties of interest and identity with the Continent:

> England is, in effect, insular, maritime, linked through its trade, markets and food supply to very diverse and often very distant countries. Its activities are essentially industrial and commercial,

and only slightly agricultural. It has, throughout its work, very marked and original customs and traditions. In short, the nature, structure and economic context of England differ profoundly from those of the other States of the Continent.[27]

If Britain entered the Common Market, she would not only bring herself as an alien element, but would seek to introduce as well the other countries of her free-trade area, along with her many dependencies and special relations around the world. There would be little chance for a coherent common policy from such a heterogeneous assemblage. True to his nationalist position, de Gaulle argued that consensus had its limits:

> It is foreseeable that the cohesion of all its members, who would be very numerous and very diverse, would not hold for long and that in the end there would appear a colossal Atlantic Community under American dependence and leadership which would soon completely swallow up the European Community.
>
> This is an assumption that can be perfectly justified in the eyes of some, but it is not at all what France wanted to do and what France is doing, which is a strictly European construction.[28]

Despite his opposition to all federalist schemes, de Gaulle continued to profess an ardent devotion to the cause of European unity. It was time, he felt, to start building a genuine European political authority.[29] Far too much time had been lost already in chasing chimeras. But the building of Europe had to begin with those institutions which existed, which enjoyed popular allegiance, and which had the authority to act—in short, with the national states. The states were:

> . . . in truth, certainly very different from one another, each of which has its own spirit, its own history, its own language, its own misfortunes, glories and ambitions; but these States are the only entities that have the right to order and the authority to act. To imagine that something can be built that would be effective for action and that would be approved by the peoples outside and above the States—this is a dream.[30]

In 1961, in the "Fouchet Plan," de Gaulle proposed the same scheme he had been suggesting since the war, a confederal Europe of States.[31] The heads of state or government would meet regularly, as would various ministers. Commissions of national rather than supranational civil servants would parallel the "economic commission" in Brussels in the fields of politics, defense, and culture. The European Parliament could extend the scope of its discussions to the full range of European politics. In three years' time the whole apparatus would be reviewed and perfected. In the original proposal de Gaulle included his old idea of a popular referendum asking the people of the Six to legitimize the new European confederal structure. But the vote was dropped because of strong opposition.[32]

The negotiations were tortuous and it remains difficult to discover exactly what happened. At one point everyone is said to have agreed but Holland; at another de Gaulle is said to have submitted a far less conciliatory new draft. Partisans of a federal Europe were worried that the new institutions, without a supranational civil service, would undermine the existing supranational bodies and be a step away from rather than towards European unity. The Common Market Executive in Brussels was unenthusiastic. Partisans of Atlantic unity were fearful of defense planning outside the framework of NATO. The whole question was immensely complicated by Britain's pending application to join the Common Market. The Dutch took the position that they would not agree to the Fouchet Plan unless the British were admitted to the negotiations.[33]

In any case the Fouchet Plan failed in the spring of 1962. Further progress towards European political unity has not proved possible in spite of several attempts by others to propose arrangements more or less along the lines of the Fouchet Plan.[34] The general principles of the plan are embodied in the Franco-German Treaty of 1963.[35] That special relationship has not been a notable success and casts suspicion on the efficacy of the confederal institutions de Gaulle proposes for the rest of Europe.

To an outside observer it is often striking how close de Gaulle's position can be to that of the ardent federalists or of the Common Market Commission itself. Intelligent partisans of Europe presumably should applaud de Gaulle's indispensable role in advancing economic integration. His criticism both of the piecemeal approach of the Communities and of their lack of a democratic base is acknowledged by a great many federalists. His resistance to British schemes for a free-trade area and his veto of British application to the Common Market was based on principles normally cherished by the advocates of a strongly integrated Europe. His insistence that America should be an ally but not a master finds many a responsive chord among European enthusiasts.

The inveterate and mounting hostility between de Gaulle and the partisans of federalist Europe seems to be explained less by their stands on particular issues than by their profound lack of sympathy for each other's fundamental political views. The two groups cannot find a common identity. They do not now belong to the same Europe and perhaps they never will. All their differences seem to gather around the question of the state—what it takes to have one, what institutions it needs to be effective, what its role must be in the world at large. De Gaulle's nationalist views seem to place him forever out of sympathy with the federalists and they with him. De Gaulle's views on the state, in turn, are at the center of his whole philosophy of politics—of the ideas he has been nurturing and preaching all his life.

3.

Few men in politics have gone to such lengths to explain their fundamental principles. De Gaulle has never been a professional politician concerned with the management of power as an art in itself. He is essentially a man driven by ideas, a reformer and teacher. With his elegant but simple prose and his slow, reasoning delivery, he lectures the people of France as if he were his father, Henri de Gaulle, at the Ecole Fontanes, or the young Captain de Gaulle at St. Cyr.[36] Again and again, de Gaulle recalls the same grand themes, most of which have remained remarkably constant for over thirty years.

It can be said that much of de Gaulle's fundamental view of things was set before the Second World War. He wrote four books in the years between the wars: *Discord among the Enemy* (1924), *The Edge of the Sword* (1932), *Towards a Professional Army* (1934), and *France and Her Army* (1938).[37] All four deal with military questions but in the broadest possible sense. Together they form a reasonably complete view of de Gaulle's over-all philosophy and its relation to politics. A detailed analysis of his ideas and the intellectual forces which influenced them would probably be a book in itself. There are, however, three main themes in his writings which it would be well to pause and consider: the inevitability of struggle and conflict in human affairs, the consequent need for individuals and societies to have will, discipline, and vision if they are to flourish in a contentious world, and finally the realization that there are certain cold rules which govern human affairs and which if denied will eventually crush even the greatest genius and enthusiasm.

The first principle, ceaseless struggle and competition, de Gaulle finds in the very nature of man. It haunts all human relations and mocks all utopian dreams for a peaceful world without struggle:

> But, hope though we may, what reason have we for thinking that passion and self-interest, the root cause of armed conflict in men and in nations, will cease to operate; that anyone will willingly surrender what he has or not try to get what he wants; in short, that human nature will ever become something other than it is? Is it really likely that the present balance of power will remain unchanged so long as the small want to become great, the strong to dominate the weak, the old to live on? [38]

De Gaulle's world is crowded with forces struggling to live and grow. Competition, death, and tragedy are the natural outcome of vitality. Only constant effort allows men and societies to flourish and assert their potential. To relax is to invite decay. It is de Gaulle's heroic pessimism that doubtless accounts for much of his sometimes harsh and malevolent austerity. It also explains his moral pride in belonging to the profession of arms.

In de Gaulle's view, armies are essential to civilization. Organized communities suffer, both inside and out, from the same inescapable contentiousness that is inseparable from life itself. Civilization requires the harnessing of power to maintain external security and internal law and order. Only power can preserve the necessary conditions within which a people can exercise the gentle talents. "In whatever direction the world may move, it will never be able to do without the final arbitrament of arms." [39] Wars are the price which man has paid for progress. Thus soldiering, the effective employment of force, is a noble and indispensable profession:

> The self-sacrifice of individuals for the sake of the community, suffering made glorious—those two things which are the basic elements of the profession of arms—respond to both our moral and aesthetic concepts. The noblest teachings of philosophy and religion have found no higher ideals. [40]

But force employed without policy, without any clear end in view, is merely stupid brutality:

> But, if force is necessary to build a state, on the other hand, the strain of going to war is only worthwhile in pursuit of a policy. As long as the country was covered by feudal underbrush, much blood flowed on the barren sands.[41]

Like his hero Clemenceau, the young de Gaulle believed war too important to be left to generals. Military strategy was ever meant to be subordinate to the ends dictated by politics; armies were meant to serve states. It was the function of the state to cultivate and coordinate the forces of a society towards preserving the national interest in the international world. Ultimately, a state depended on its own resources. A nation often needed allies, but it could not finally transfer to others the burden of guarding its interests. In the world of states, power was the final common denominator determining who should prosper and who should perish. A nation which retired from asserting its interests would see those interests neglected. A state which lacked the power to assert itself would not be treated kindly by events.

No state could be effective without strong leadership. In times of stress above all, a firm and unyielding leader was needed to embody the general interest and assert it over particular interests and partial views. Without such leadership, the door was opened to the forces of disorder, coherence vanished from the national effort, and the energies of the nation—no longer summoned to the service of a directing will—were dissipated while public morale collapsed. That was how de Gaulle analyzed Germany's fall in World War I. Without a Clemenceau to mobilize and direct its forces, the nation disintegrated.[42]

Leadership came only from one source: strong men of insight and character, eager to take responsibility for events. The young de Gaulle spelled out his views on the character of the leader in a remarkable series of lectures delivered at the War College in

1927 [43] and subsequently published in 1932 as *Le Fil de l'Epée.* The lectures were arranged by Marshall Pétain as a mark of favor for his protégé, the brilliant and radical young officer whose career, like his own a generation earlier, had been dogged by the dislike of the entrenched military bureaucracy.

The young captain discoursed on greatness.[44] These were hard days for authority, he observed. An elite could rule effectively only when its right to command was accepted willingly. But the old formulas which had endowed hierarchy with legitimacy were now worn out. It was not that the need for leaders had disappeared. The need for leadership in human affairs was permanent. The masses always craved direction and not without reason, for "deprived of a master, they soon suffer from the results of their own turbulence." [45] The stability and progress of modern society, so completely the result of organization, depended all the more on leadership and obedience. Modern leaders who did manage to get themselves accepted by the masses were obeyed with a blindness never before granted even to the most legitimate of princes. But within a skeptical and disoriented society, authority had to be based on personal prestige rather than rank. "What the masses once granted to birth or office, they now give to those who can assert themselves." [46]

Prestige was built mostly on "feeling, suggestion, and impression"—"a natural aptitude which defies analysis." Some men had from birth "the quality of exuding authority" which was a gift like that of the artist.[47] Like all such natural gifts, it had to be refined and disciplined before it was effective. Leadership required both strong drive and extreme self-discipline. The leader's life was lonely and often tormented. Ordinary men externalized and dissipated their inner passions by talk. The great leader conserved the intensity of his energies by silence and mastered them by meditation and will. The great leader was, above all, a solitary man who meditated. Only by aloofness could he maintain his authority; only by profound study and reflection could he come to understand the nature of the events he sought to dominate. For de Gaulle's leader, as for Plato's philosopher-king, the great temptation was solitude—withdrawal completely into the world of meditation.[48]

Leadership consisted not only in persuading men to follow, but in having somewhere to lead them. Obedience was never easy. Great leaders were often obnoxious because of their pride, hardness, and cunning. They were forgiven only because of the results they achieved:

> The question of virtue does not arise. The perfection preached in the Gospels never yet built up an empire. Every man of action has a strong dose of egotism, pride, hardness, and cunning. But all those things will be forgiven him, indeed, they will be regarded as high qualities, if he can make of them the means to achieve great ends.[49]

To retain his prestige the leader needed two fundamental qualities: the ability to command effectively and a superior insight into the nature of events. These two essential talents both needed constant effort to develop and maintain. To lead required first of all mastering the techniques of command. At the bottom of all these techniques lay the real basis of obedience—the leader's ability to penetrate into the wills of his followers so that they came to identify his commands with their wishes, his aspirations with their own:

> If he is to have a genuine and effective hold on his men, he must know how to make their wills part and parcel of his own, and so to inspire them that they will look upon the task assigned to them as something of their own choosing.[50]

The greatest loyalty came to those leaders whose identification with a noble cause lent grandeur to the humblest of their followers:

> It is essential that the plan on which the leader has concentrated all his faculties shall bear the mark of grandeur. It must, indeed,

respond to the cravings felt by men who, imperfect themselves, seek perfection in the end they are called upon to serve.[51]

The great leader aroused the moral energies of lesser men and directed them to heights which they could never reach without him:

Thus, by satisfying the secret desires of men's hearts, by providing compensation for the cramped conditions of their lives, he will capture their imagination, and, even should he fall by the way, will retain, in their eyes, the prestige of those heights to which he did his best to lead them.[52]

The leader, responsible to the fervent loyalty of his followers, had especial need for a realistic policy based on a perceptive and balanced insight into the world as it really was. That profound insight required a superior mixture of intelligence and intuition:

Our intelligence can furnish us with the theoretic, general abstract knowledge of what is, but only instinct can give the practical, particular, and concrete *feel* of it. Without the cooperation of the intelligence there can be no logical reasoning, no informed judgment. But without the reinforcement of instinct there can be no profundity of perception and no creative urge. Instinct is the faculty in our make-up which brings us into close contact with nature. Thanks to it, we can strike deeply into the order of things, and participate in whatever obscure harmony may be found there. It is by instinct that man discerns the reality of the conditions which surround him, and feels a corresponding impulsion.[53]

"Instinct" was especially important to the man of action because, as the philosopher Bergson observed: "Our reasoning faculty, so sure of itself when it ranges over the world of inanimate objects, finds itself ill at ease in this new field of action." [54] Intelligence relied on the assumption that the same causes would always produce the same results; nothing, de Gaulle argued, illustrated better than a military campaign the practical inadequacy of pure intelligence. The commander dealt with an infinite number of variables—the enemy, the terrain, his own troops and equipment. Few of these elements had any constant value. The complexities of battle defied a logic based only on recurring patterns of cause and effect. "The swift-moving and muddied flow of circumstance can no more be imprisoned in its mesh than water can be caught and held in a fishing net." [55]

Intelligence was vitally important, of course, to a military commander. It provided the facts of a situation in advance and clarified and assigned their relative significance. Through intelligence, the leader's mind built a conceptual picture of the flow of events which gave him purchase for acting upon those events. Furthermore, rational intelligence, by organizing the army into standard trained units, allowed the leader to control the actions of an immense number of men and machines with great precision. Intelligence was always indispensable—in preparing a plan of action and in perfecting the means for carrying it out—but it was not enough. Instinct was equally necessary if the leader was to penetrate to the obscure harmony which lay behind events and be able to separate the essential from the peripheral.

Military doctrine which misunderstood this relationship between intelligence and intuition either became excessively dogmatic and prescribed exact rules for every conceivable situation or excessively irrational and abandoned rational calculation entirely for *esprit*.[56]

De Gaulle's writings on the nature of command reveal his views on the nature of truth and leadership generally. Intellect was vital but had to be joined by instinct—a gift which was not granted equally to all men, which could be refined but not imparted by education, and which had to be exercised alone in meditation. It was not surprising that de Gaulle compared the mental processes of the commander with those of the creative artist. Each sought in his own field to penetrate to the inner spirit of events. Each followed a "method" employing both intellect and inspiration.

These notions of truth and how it is perceived are not, it

scarcely needs saying, peculiar to de Gaulle. They represent a way of looking at truth, present in Western thought since Plato, which enjoyed an important revival among German and English Romantic Idealists in the nineteenth century. The revival came later to France, but it found one of its major figures in the philosopher Henri Bergson (1859–1941). De Gaulle knew Bergson and quoted him on a number of occasions. There are a number of interesting parallels in their writings and a knowledge of Bergson helps to explain several points in de Gaulle.[57]

In *Creative Evolution* (1907), Bergson saw an endless changing world where both species and individuals struggled to survive, express themselves, and evolve their further potential. In the struggle to live, it was the brain and nervous system of the animal that coordinated its forces, much as de Gaulle's state summoned and directed the forces of the nation. Bergson was much concerned, moreover, with the distinctive functions appropriate to intelligence and instinct. It was characteristic of the intellect that it sought to break down wholes into parts—parts which could be treated as units to be labelled, arranged, compared, and perhaps controlled—much as an armed horde might be organized into the uniform and manageable parts of a modern disciplined army. Seen from the vantage point of the intellect, the world was composed of innumerable units arranged according to certain uniform laws. Action was a series of discrete events taking place through time—itself a creation of the intellect.

Bergson argued that the intellect, by its dismemberment of the living whole into abstracted parts, by its disintegration of a single act into tiny separate events, invariably gave a distorted picture of reality. For the events were determined by vital energies seeking to express themselves. The intellect focused only on the outward effects of these forces, but never could perceive the forces themselves.

Bergson explained himself best by a vivid metaphor. A hand moving through iron filings displaced them in a single sweeping action. The intellect with its partial vision could see only the filings, the matter affected, but not the force itself, not the hand. The intellect thus broke down the single act of the hand into a series of almost innumerable separate actions taking place over time, a heap of apparently unrelated phenomena. It could not see that the action was caused by the single sweep of the hand, not by the endless complex interactions of the filings one with another. Hence the intellect, seeking the cause of biological evolution, characteristically sought for a mechanism which explained evolution by small, accidental increments and overlooked entirely the real cause, the "vital force" which impelled a species to its development. To find the vital force at the base of events required more than intellect; it required an intuitive instinct as well. This instinct related man to the great forces which lay behind actions and gave him, as well, an introspective knowledge of the unconscious springs of his own being. Instinct, in short, endowed the conscious mind with insights that intellect alone could never give. Only when the two were fused—a process requiring intense meditation—could man gain consciousness of the true nature of himself and the outside world. Thus man, in a manner of speaking, could escape from time because he saw the whole in each part, the end in the beginning. He entered into the world of "duration." Furthermore, his knowledge of the real forces at work gave him the ability to intervene effectively in the chain of events.

These perceptions were limited to the relative few who had the will and training to exercise them properly. The necessary insights could never come from the mechanical accumulation of information garnered by many. Those materials might be essential, but never sufficient without a gifted mind to assemble them and penetrate to their essence. While profound knowledge never came from inspiration alone, neither could it be arrived at in committee. Only the intense concentration of the inspired man who had mastered his material could lead to true insight.

The Bergsonian view of reality could be made to have obvious political implications. Bergson's whole way of looking at truth and its perception almost inevitably called for an elite of leaders. The insight necessary for the great scientist, artist, historian, or military leader was not common to all men. In these matters, the common man followed and did not hope to lead. The capability of the whole social organism to flourish might be seen to depend on whether there were enough such leaders spread throughout the society.

De Gaulle took a Bergsonian view and integrated it into his political philosophy of leadership and the state. His notions of leadership meant that he would regard all committee governments as weak governments, that he would be dissatisfied with any state that lacked a genuine chief, that he would, in short, deplore the Third Republic with its weak and plural executive and would hope someday to see installed in France a presidential system which allowed scope for a strong leader with vision.

For de Gaulle, strong personal leadership did not imply monolithic unity in the society. In *Le Fil de l'Epée* he proposed a sort of federalism of leaders. For society to prosper, he argued, there had to be institutions which trained leaders and allowed them to function at all levels of common life. Society could be healthy only when it was filled with men of exceptional vision eager to take responsibility and stamp their vision upon events. If the leadership were genuine, there would be no need to fear anarchy. The strong leader preferred ardent and strong-willed subordinates. He would know how to control their excesses and channel their ardor.[58]

De Gaulle's concept of the leader suggests another major philosopher with whose world view he might appear to have more than a passing affinity, Friedrich Nietzsche (1844–1900). De Gaulle discussed Nietzsche at some length in *Discord among the Enemy*. Nietzsche was above all concerned with the great man—the superman gifted with superior vitality and insight who achieved self-mastery over powerful passions by an even stronger will. Nietzsche's hero remained aloof, lonely, and tormented. His whole life was a noble work of art, shaped by his own taste and will. He was a luxuriant and beautiful plant flowering in a lawless and incoherent jungle. His life was its own justification; his perfection the only valid rule. Lesser men were merely the material at hand for the expression of his own genius.[59]

There was much that de Gaulle must have found sympathetic. But de Gaulle never suggested in his writing that the leader was an end in himself and that other men were irrelevant. On the contrary, the leader was always justified by the good he did for the society. That was the source of his authority and de Gaulle never claimed any other.

Nietzsche's contemptuous indifference to the popular herd was not, of course, an appropriate position for a democratic politician, and even de Gaulle might have been expected to repress his enthusiasm for Nietzsche's intense loathing for the common man.[60] But prudence aside, a fundamental strand in de Gaulle's thought clearly opposes Nietzsche. Along with all his Romantic ideas and in particular his emphasis on the importance of will, there remains in de Gaulle a healthy French respect for *mesure*, for those "rules of the classical order. . . . that sense of balance, of the possible, of measure, which alone makes lasting and fruitful the works of energy." [61]

The most ardent genius and enthusiasm could not for long fly in the face of reason and balance. The attempt might be glorious, but the disastrous results could be foreknown. That was the profound lesson, in *France and Her Army*, that de Gaulle drew from the stupendous career of Napoleon. De Gaulle could not help but admire the leader whose genius fused and animated all the forces of France. But it was certain from the start that the Emperor's essentially boundless ambitions would lead to an "infernal cycle of battles" and inevitable defeat.[62] De Gaulle's ambivalent admiration is contained in his own summary of Napoleon's career: "Tragic revenge of measure, just wrath of reason; but superhuman prestige of genius and marvelous valor of arms." [63]

De Gaulle's appreciation for measure, the third major theme of his prewar writings, was at heart aesthetic. *Mesure,* for de Gaulle as for Nietzsche, was a particularly French virtue. The French had a culture which treasured finesse and precision, while their neighbors the Germans were troubled by an abundant but chaotic vitality:

> In a French garden, no tree tries to stifle the others by its shadow, the flowerbeds make the best of being geometrically arranged, the pond does not yearn to cascade, the statues do not seek to thrust themselves up individually for admiration. Occasionally, one senses a noble melancholy. Perhaps it comes from the feeling that each element, if isolated, could have shone more. But this would have been to the detriment of the whole, and the stroller is glad for the rule which gives to the garden its magnificent harmony.[64]

De Gaulle's classical taste was equally pronounced in matters of military strategy. He foresaw that modern warfare would become dominated by professional technicians and that the days of the old-fashioned nation in arms were limited. It was a change he welcomed. For aesthetic as well as humanitarian reasons, de Gaulle greatly preferred small elite professional armies who employed carefully measured force with precision and style to achieve limited ends rather than the massively destructive, undisciplined, incoherent, and lumbering warfare of peoples.[65] World War I represented for de Gaulle the nadir of modern history.[66] Reason had completely lost control of force and the destruction exceeded beyond all measure the proper ends of the states. Not only was the fighting in itself a nightmare of incoherent slaughter, but it reflected the general madness of European politics. The states of Europe had forgotten that higher logic which dictated their general interdependence. Instead, states were pursuing unreasonable ambitions which could only result in gain for no one and ruin for all.

The notion of the higher interdependence of states, especially the states of Europe, was a continuing theme in prewar de

Gaulle, tied closely to the general emphasis on *mesure*. De Gaulle observed in *Towards a Professional Army*:

Finally, the ubiquity of wealth, the entanglement of interests, the osmosis of ideas have created among peoples an interdependence which fixes by necessity bounds on their ambitions. Everyone has observed that the misfortune of some, if it exceeds a certain degree, does not result in the good fortune of others. And each in particular, if confident of his superiority, does not aspire to omnipotence.[67]

Interdependence, of course, did not mean that a state could cease to compete with others and live in some effortlessly harmonious system. In an interdependent system each state was still expected to promote vigorously its own interests, but to calculate and pursue them in a rational manner. The neglect by a state of its own position, either from mistaken altruism or laziness, would very likely cause harm to all states in general. For the higher interest of states demanded a balance of power. Once the balance was allowed to deteriorate, the logic of interdependence ceased to impose clear limits to ambition. Sooner or later the situation would tempt someone to grand adventures and in the end everyone would pay. Napoleon III's ideological preoccupations, for example, led him to allow and even aid Austria's defeat in Italy and Germany. His disregard of France's power position, his flouting of the "cold rules" of strategy and politics left France in 1870 with a powerful enemy and no friends. Victorious Germany became strong enough to dream of hegemony and World War I was the catastrophic result.[68]

Of all the regimes France had endured, de Gaulle found the *Ancien Régime* the most acceptable to his taste, precisely because what he saw as its sense of measure preserved the independence and grandeur of France in the most economical and pragmatic fashion possible:

The policy of the *Ancien Régime* is that of circumstance; careful to avoid abstractions, but savoring of realities, preferring the useful to the sublime, the opportune to the resounding, searching, for each particular problem, not the ideal solution, but the practical one, not very scrupulous as to the means, but grand, all the same, by the observation of the right proportion between the object pursued and the forces of the state.[69]

It was the *Ancien Régime*, in short, which best honored the three great political themes of de Gaulle's prewar writings: competition, leadership, and measure.

Some knowledge of de Gaulle's general views is extremely useful in understanding his politics, although such knowledge is not a key to determining his reactions to every situation. He is not a computer for whom it can reasonably be predicted that if certain things go in, certain things will come out. De Gaulle's policies are sometimes of remarkably long duration, but they can change with disconcerting swiftness. His basic view of the world does not change. One does not necessarily find in his past the clue to what he will say in the future, but rather the key to understanding what he is saying in the present.

The simultaneous coexistence in de Gaulle's world view of conflict, will, and order make him an extraordinarily complex figure. It is this tension which has prompted some biographers to describe him as baroque.[70] The label is apt. The baroque loved order but knew that it could be imposed on a chaotic world only by the superhuman will and grandeur of a great artist. Of course de Gaulle's intellect, his immense knowledge, his sensitivity, and above all his imagination make him a great creative artist in the world of politics. What remains to be seen is whether, in so volatile a medium as politics, he can leave a monument worthy of his genius.

4.

The Second World War changed de Gaulle's life from contemplation to action. On the whole, his experience in the war elaborated rather than changed his earlier ideas. The performance of the Third Republic, both before and at the moment of crisis, only confirmed his worst fears about the nature of that regime. For years de Gaulle had conducted a campaign to reform the army so that France could act effectively, first to prevent the German threat, later to meet it honorably. To the last, the regime proved incapable of acting effectively.[71] Even when Reynaud, the politician who had championed de Gaulle's military ideas, became Prime Minister in late 1939, it seemed that nothing could be done to overcome the monumental inertia of the army.[72] For de Gaulle, the army only reflected the regime itself. Neither was capable of movement. When the supreme test came, both disintegrated:

It has to be said that at the supreme moment the regime offered to the head of the last government of the Third Republic nothing to fall back upon. Assuredly many of the men in office looked upon capitulation with horror. But the authorities, shattered by the disaster for which they felt themselves responsible, did not react at all. At the time when they were faced by the problem on which, for France, all the present and all the future depended, Parliament did not sit, the Government showed itself incapable of adopting as a body a decisive solution, and the President of the Republic abstained from raising his voice, even within the Cabinet, to express the supreme interest of the country. In reality this annihilation of the state was at the bottom of the national tragedy. By the light of the thunderbolt the regime was revealed, in its ghastly infirmity, as having no proportion and no relation to the defence, honour, and independence of France.[73]

The root of the Third Republic's weakness, according to de Gaulle, was a constitution which made proper leadership for the French state impossible.[74] To begin with, the regime was governed by parties—groups who, by definition, represented only particular segments of society and thus were limited both in their conceptions of the national welfare and in their popular support. In such a system, leadership invariably fell to the men who were most skilled in adding together particular interests rather than in seeing the good of the nation as a whole or rallying the people to it. Furthermore, the inevitable requirements of coalition government made any Prime Minister's hold on office so precarious that he never was free to strike out boldly to resolve the greatest national problems.[75] The structure was such that no man could exercise coherent leadership. Policy was a monstrosity which came out of no one's mind in particular, but was a patchwork of the special interests momentarily in power. It was a system which feared greatness and positively discouraged men of strong character.

Finally, it was a system which denied the state any satisfactory contact with the people. The parties with their "dogmas"—intellectual constructions pursued for ideological exercise—had become increasingly abstracted from the general character of the society and culture. Parties made contact with their public only at the level of the special economic interests of their patrons and clients. Thus the Third Republic embraced a constitutional system which denied every possibility for effective leadership. The results, as de Gaulle saw them, could only follow naturally. It was the function of the state to lead—to provide the directing brain to the national society. When the society lacked a strong state, it could not meet the challenges of a demanding environment. The nation could not summon and focus its energies, even in the worst moments of supreme peril. France, like some vast mindless dinosaur of the prehistoric era, was ready for extinction.

As de Gaulle saw it, France stood in great danger after Vichy's capitulation of having no state at all; and without a state to represent her interests and focus her efforts, France would never emerge from her degradation. Pétain's great crime, in de Gaulle's eyes, was that he made it difficult, by confusing the loyalties of Frenchmen, for a new state to be formed.[76] De Gaulle's whole wartime crusade sought not merely to arm some French auxiliaries against the Germans but, above all, to reconstitute around himself the French state:

> What was the good of supplying with auxiliaries the forces of another power? No! For the effort to be worth while, it was essential to bring back into the war not merely some Frenchmen, but France.[77]

Only thus could France ever hope to climb back up from the abyss into which she had fallen:

> At stake was not only the enemy's expulsion from her territory, but also her future as a nation and a state. Should she remain prostrate until the war's end, her faith in herself would be destroyed, and with that faith her independence as well. From the "silence of the sea" she would pass into a permanent coma, from a servitude imposed by her enemies she would decline to a subordinate position in relation to her allies. On the other hand, nothing was lost if she returned to the ranks with her unity restored. Once again the future could be safeguarded on condition that France, at the end of the drama, was a belligerent reunited by its commitment to a single central authority.[78]

De Gaulle's ambition to reconstitute the French state was at the root of his quarrels with his wartime allies. The United States in particular insisted on treating de Gaulle as the leader of a French refugee army, one of several, and not as the plenipotentiary of a sovereign state which deserved to be treated as a great power. De Gaulle was continually accused of injecting politics into military matters. To him, the whole charge was meaningless. While as a soldier he agreed that politicians should stay off the battlefield, it was a fundamental Gaullist axiom that "armies . . . are created to serve the policy of states." [79]

De Gaulle was exasperated by those who constantly urged the Free French to forego a discussion of political matters and concern themselves only with fighting the Germans: "Is there a single state in the world today which fights for the pleasure of making war? Is there a single state in the world which makes war for anything other than a political policy? Why do you want the French people to make war, suffer from war, fight, other than for a political policy?" [80] De Gaulle's Free French, in short, were not auxiliaries. The whole point of the movement was their claim to embody the French state and to be carrying on the war for France and no one else:

> Yet the Anglo-American powers never consented to deal with us as genuine allies. They never consulted us, as from government to government, on any of their intentions. By policy or expediency, they sought to make use of the French forces for goals they themselves have determined on, as if these forces belonged to them, and in justification citing the fact that they had contributed to their armament and supply. [81]

De Gaulle's experiences with the Allies confirmed his general views not only on the necessity of states, but also on the underlying competitiveness of their relations. De Gaulle fought a long and hard campaign to protect France from her friends. There were the frequent bitter quarrels with the British over French possessions in the Near East. [82] But the clash with the British was moderate compared with the profound hostility between de Gaulle and Roosevelt. From the very beginning, Roosevelt refused to recognize de Gaulle's Committee as the wartime French government. Roosevelt continued to deal with a variety of French groups, for a long time including Vichy itself and its North African extension under Darlan. When Roosevelt finally abandoned Vichy, he picked a rival French general, Giraud, and sought by American support to make him the leader of the Free French:

But, with an astonishing self-contradiction, the policy of the United States, while keeping diplomatic relations with Pétain, held aloof from Free France on the pretext that it was impossible to prejudge what government the French nation would give itself when it was liberated. At bottom, what the American policy-makers took for granted was the effacement of France. They therefore came to terms with Vichy. If, nonetheless, at certain points of the world they contemplated collaborating with this or that French authority as the struggle might dictate, they intended that this should be only by episodic and local arrangements.[83]

As several students of their relations have pointed out, de Gaulle was probably right about Roosevelt's intentions.[84] What is less often said, perhaps, is that the American President's views were based upon something more substantial than personal dislike for an upstart general who claimed to be the soul of France. Roosevelt was dreaming of a new international order in which a cooperative world organization, dominated by the United States and Russia, would police the world to prevent war in the future. Naturally Roosevelt was unenthusiastic about reviving the seemingly discredited national states of the European Continent, whose quarrels had so often brought disaster to the rest of the world and themselves. To Roosevelt, de Gaulle was a dangerous anachronism. He represented what Roosevelt was hoping to suppress in the postwar world. For de Gaulle, on the other hand, Roosevelt, beneath the patrician charm and the idealistic phrases, stood for something very old in the world, the lust for power:

Franklin Roosevelt was governed by the loftiest ambitions. His intelligence, his knowledge and his audacity gave him the ability, the powerful state of which he was the leader afforded him the means, and the war offered him the occasion to realise them. If the great nation he directed had long been inclined to isolate itself from distant enterprises and to mistrust a Europe ceaselessly lacerated by wars and revolutions, a kind of messianic impulse now swelled the American spirit and oriented it toward vast undertakings. The

United States, delighting in her resources, feeling that she no longer had within herself sufficient scope for her energies, wishing to help those who were in misery or bondage the world over, yielded in her turn to that taste for intervention in which the instinct for domination cloaked itself. It was precisely this tendency that President Roosevelt espoused. He had therefore done everything to enable his country to take part in the world conflict. He was now fulfilling his destiny, impelled as he was by the secret admonition of death.[85]

In the *Memoirs*, de Gaulle used the occasion of his journey to Washington in 1944 to dramatize the great issue that he saw at the heart of the long quarrel between Roosevelt and himself. Their conversations confirmed, he says, his long-standing belief that the American President was determined to arrange the affairs of Europe directly with Russia and over the heads of the Europeans themselves. Furthermore, he realized that Roosevelt was skeptical about the revival of Europe in general and France in particular. Nor, in de Gaulle's view, was Roosevelt in the least eager that the Europeans should revive as great powers. What Roosevelt sought, as his scheme for the United Nations made clear, was "a permanent system of intervention that he intended to institute by international law." [86] For de Gaulle it was nothing less than world government by a four-power directory dominated by America. It was the opposite swing of the American pendulum away from isolation towards imperialism. The great powers of Europe were shattered and America, fresh on the world scene with enormous resources and expansive ideological pretentions, could not be expected to resist the old temptation to boundless power. De Gaulle saw Roosevelt's grand design as nothing new in the history of states. It was America's bid for world hegemony; it was the "will to power cloaked . . . in idealism." [87]

De Gaulle realized how closely Europe and America depended on each other. But interdependence, for de Gaulle, meant not that Europe should abdicate to America, but that it should revive to the point where it could act as an effective check on non-

European pretentions to world domination. Interdependence meant a number of independent states, conscious of their mutual interests and hence cooperating closely in certain spheres—but as equals. It did not mean the domination of several states by one superpower. De Gaulle's account of his own reply to Roosevelt is worth quoting:

> "It is the West," I told President Roosevelt, "that must be restored. If it regains its balance, the rest of the world, whether it wishes to or not, will take it for an example. If it declines, barbarism will ultimately sweep everything away. Now, Western Europe, despite its dissensions and its distress, is essential to the West. Nothing can replace the value, the power, the shining examples of these ancient peoples. This is true of France above all, which of all the great nations of Europe is the only one which was, is and always will be your ally. I know that you are preparing to aid France materially, and that aid will be invaluable to her. But it is in the political realm that she must recover her vigor, her self-reliance and, consequently, her role. How can she do this if she is excluded from the organization of the great world powers and their decisions, if she loses her African and Asian territories—in short, if the settlement of the war definitively imposes upon her the psychology of the vanquished?" [88]

Roosevelt avowed his affection for France, but:

> As for the future, he was anything but convinced of the rebirth and renewal of our regime. With bitterness he described what his feelings were when before the war he watched the spectacle of our political impotence unfold before his eyes. "Even I, the President of the United States," he told me, "would sometimes find myself incapable of remembering the name of the current head of the French government. For the moment, you are there, and you see with what kind attentions my country welcomes you. But will you still be there at the tragedy's end?" [89]

De Gaulle notes in his *Memoirs:*

> The American President's remarks ultimately proved to me that, in foreign affairs, logic and sentiment do not weigh heavily in

comparison with the realities of power; that what matters is what one takes and what one can hold on to; that to regain her place, France must count only on herself. I told him this. He smiled and concluded: "We shall do what we can. But it is true that to serve France no one can replace the French people." [90]

It was a lesson that de Gaulle scarcely needed to learn.

It must have been especially bitter for de Gaulle, then and later, that Roosevelt's estimate of France appeared only too just. It was what the General himself had said of the French state under the Third Republic. And, as Roosevelt accurately foresaw, the postwar French would return to their old ways. De Gaulle would soon be out of power. The regime of the parties would return. The French state would be too weak for de Gaulle's notions of France's role as a great power. The French, no longer summoned to grandeur, would lose their taste for greatness and indulge themselves in sterile old arguments and comfortable old quarrels. In the grip of a sort of neurasthenia, they would gradually relax into the status of an American protectorate, depending upon a protection which, in de Gaulle's view, was not likely to remain reliable.[91] That was what Roosevelt predicted; that was what de Gaulle came bitterly to believe was happening.

The alternative, as de Gaulle constantly proposed it, was for Frenchmen to continue the arduous struggle for national self-renewal until they again became masters of their own fate. The struggle would not be easy; it would require enormous effort, discipline, intelligence, courage, and audacity. These were the qualities which a great people would have to find in themselves. But they would have to be summoned by a great leader. It has been de Gaulle's mission to be that leader. Since that fateful day on the eighteenth of June, 1940, the self-appointed conscience of France has never ceased to preach that same message: "Whatever happens, the flame of French resistance must not and will not go out." [92] The theme of his famous wartime broadcasts remains his theme today.[93]

5.

Long before the liberation, de Gaulle began planning France's postwar renewal. Most of the groups around him came to be almost as concerned with building a new France as with driving out the Germans. The Resistance produced a ferment of studies purporting to map the new future.[94] However much they differed among themselves, they all shared in the ardent belief that the vigor and unity which animated the Free French and the Resistance would sweep over liberated France and give the nation a new birth of vitality and moral strength. A new elite was forming to lead France out of the self-indulgent confusion of the old regime.

By the time de Gaulle returned to France, he was ready with his program for restoring the country to greatness. Domestically, his theme was leadership and renewal; externally, independence. De Gaulle "placed the social question first among all those the government had to resolve." "The century's great debate," he realized, was whether "the working classes would be the victim or the beneficiary of technical progress." A revived France would require a great program of economic and fiscal reform. "I was convinced that without profound and rapid changes in this realm, there would be no lasting order." [95]

The changes were truly rapid and far-reaching. Many banks and certain large firms like Renault were nationalized. The government took over the instruments to manage the economy, and the "Plan" was established with Jean Monnet as its first chairman. A vast welfare and social security program changed profoundly the conditions and prospects of the working class.

Few other men in French history have brought such radical reform peacefully, though it was typical of de Gaulle that he should justify his program on the ground that healing social divisions and increasing production would greatly expand the external power of the state.[96] By 1946 he found himself too revolutionary for many of his wartime followers and for the great majority of French politicians:

> On the whole, seeing around me these courageous colleagues of such good will, I felt myself full of esteem for all and of friendship for many. But also, probing their souls, I reached a point where I asked myself if among all those who spoke of revolution I was not, in truth, the only revolutionary." [97]

The great showdown between de Gaulle and the reviving politicians came over the new constitution. De Gaulle's ideas on leadership demanded that it be radically new. Above all, he hoped to avoid a return to the old parliamentary system with its familiar inability either to formulate policy or to rally the people. De Gaulle's definitive statement on the constitution remains his speech at Bayeux in June, 1946. The speech, in fact, is a grand summary of all the Gaullist themes of struggle, leadership, and measure. The war, de Gaulle began, saw the unexpected rebirth of the defeated French state. With victory assured, the work of rehabilitation would have to go on if France were to avoid a return to the disastrous weakness which led to her abysmal fall in 1940. France, which had in "only twice the normal span of a man's life . . . been invaded seven times and . . . had thirteen régimes" could never hope to escape from danger.[98] The end of the war had not brought real peace; "the times are very hard and very dangerous!" [99]

To survive in such a world, de Gaulle argued, the French needed a strong state. "Our whole history is the alternation of the immense sorrows of a divided people, and the fruitful grandeur of a free nation grouped under the aegis of a strong state." [100] A strong presidential system was the only way to avoid the fatal oscillation between anarchy and despotism. The great danger of a weak government was that it "leads inevitably to the disaffection of its citizens towards its Constituion." [101] Efficient administration was vital in the modern world, and when it was lacking the citizenry began impatiently to crave a strong government at any price. The price was generally dictatorship. Such had been the lamentable pattern of the First, Second, and Third Republics of France, as well as the republican regimes of Germany, Italy, and Spain. Dictatorship might restore order and even public morale. "But it is the destiny of all dictators to go too far in what they undertake." Their lack of measure makes disaster inevitable: "The great edifice collapses in blood and ruin, and the nation, broken, finds itself in a worse position than it had been when the great adventure began." [102]

De Gaulle failed to get his new constitution and resigned rather than assume personal power. That game, he felt, would have ended badly. Lasting institutions could never spring from a *coup d'état*. He preferred to retire with his moral capital intact. It is generally thought that he expected to be called back soon. If so, he miscalculated badly. The restored party regime endured until 1958 when it broke down before the Algerian crisis and the imminent danger of civil war. But after his long wait, de Gaulle was at last given a free hand to establish what he had long been preaching, a strong presidential regime.

This is not the place for a lengthy analysis of the Gaullist constitution of 1958, its development, or its prospects. The chief power in the new constitution is held by the President, now to be elected by universal suffrage. The Prime Minister, while responsible to the Assembly, has in recent years become the chief lieutenant of the President. Since 1962, the functioning of the institutions has been greatly affected by the presence of a loyal Gaullist majority in the Assembly.

De Gaulle spoke of his system as establishing the separation of powers; what has resulted in practice is that the legislative and executive powers have become amalgamated in the President. It is he who formulates policy and carries it out. Elected by universal suffrage, the President is meant to represent the general will of the whole people, while the Assembly is seen as an aggregate of the particular interests of the country. It is only fitting, it is argued, that the President should hold the initiative in making policy. No real policy can come from the mere addition of several interests.

But the Parliament persists as a major element in the Gaullist system. It still has power—if not to lead, at least to refuse to follow. The legislature can debate policies and summon the ministers to defend them. The legislature can even withdraw its confidence and bring down the Prime Minister. The President must then either choose a new minister acceptable to the Assembly or, if there is a basic conflict in policy, appeal directly to the people, either by calling for new Parliamentary elections or a referendum on a particular issue. But as long as the President has the confidence of the people, he exercises the decisive power in the state.

Even with de Gaulle's towering prestige and with a majority in the Parliament, however, laws are not passed without effort. Governments have fallen.[103] Above all, Parliament has the freedom to criticize and to demand an answer to its criticisms. And the Assembly is not without resources in appealing to public opinion. If France is a presidential dictatorship, it nevertheless has a most remarkably critical press. If Frenchmen do not hear, it is not because the voices of the opposition have been silenced.[104]

It is not accurate to say that Parliament and its parties have no genuine function in the Gaullist constitution, either as it operates or as it was conceived. Though they may not decide issues, they inform both the public and the President. They express, if in an exaggerated form, the particular interests of those diverse and contending groups—the "spiritual families" which make up the nation. They provide the raw material out of which the leader can fashion his decisions. Parliament provides the leader with the "intelligence;" it reminds the President of what is possible and discourages that taste for the measureless which has been the downfall of so many great men. Its pressing of special interests is essential; the general interest should transcend particular interests, not destroy them.

De Gaulle's descriptions of his Cabinet meetings, during the war and after, illustrate his views on the process of presidential leadership. At the beginning of each session, the President defined the problems. Each man spoke freely. There were disagreements. In the end, de Gaulle sought to summarize and resolve. Generally, he says, the discussion itself produced a consensus.[105]

De Gaulle's constitution shows the influence of a number of French theorists, above all that of his first Prime Minister, Michel Debré, who saw it as a combination of monarchy and democracy.[106] It might almost have been invented by Disraeli.[107] It marks the end not of Parliament but of government by Parliament—of that oligarchic regime within which, it might be argued, the elite had grown too remote from the needs and sympathies of the people. Political power has passed to a modern king who reigns because, and only as long as, he serves the interests and sympathies of the people. Monarchy and democracy have combined. The other great constitutional principle, oligarchy, has found its place in the burgeoning elite of mandarins who will become, true to their nature, the most effective check on the daily power of both king and people.[108]

Whether the Gaullist constitution represents an important evolutionary step towards a workable modern form of constitutional government or a retrogression to Bonapartism or fascism will long be debated. Much, of course, depends upon how de Gaulle ends his career and, above all, on how he arranges the succession. De Gaulle may despise parties, but it is difficult to see how orderly succession can be managed without them.[109]

The majority of Frenchmen today are believed to support not only de Gaulle but his constitution.[110] Whether the regime lasts will depend, as such matters no doubt generally do, on the good luck and good sense of the French people and their politicians. In any event, whatever the future may hold it must be admitted that de Gaulle has finally achieved his first great aim. France today has a strong state, capable of making difficult decisions and rallying the people behind them. Indeed, the Gaullists often boast that France is the only country in Europe with a government.

6.

The second part of de Gaulle's grand effort to revive French power, his diplomatic campaign, has been no less true to his basic political tenets nor any less revolutionary and controversial. Its basic aim has been simple: to preserve the independence of France. While de Gaulle has never ceased to acknowledge the necessity of the Western Alliance as long as the Soviet Union is a threat, he has never stopped trying, within the Alliance itself, to undermine American hegemony and to gain a greater role for France. To give France greater weight, he has sought close alliances with England and Germany and even flirted with Russia. He has tried to make his country the leader of a European confederation which could somehow greatly increase the power of France without destroying her independence. Increasingly in recent years, he has cultivated French influence in the Third World.

The essential problem of French diplomacy, in de Gaulle's view, has been to enjoy effective American protection against Russia while preserving for France her independence and eventual freedom of action. That policy has never changed. Thus de Gaulle continues to the present day to affirm the absolute necessity of the Western Alliance even while his government consistently sabotages every American attempt to integrate European forces under an effective central control. That control means, as far as de Gaulle is concerned, American domination of Europe.

De Gaulle's Atlantic policy invariably appears puzzling, idiotic, or sinister to those who cannot imagine why anyone except a communist would want to be independent of the United States or to those for whom almost any form of international integration is an end in itself. But de Gaulle does pose a reasonable question: why should France give up its independence to anyone, America included? As far as de Gaulle is concerned, NATO is an alliance and nothing more. He sees alliances as the means for a state to maintain independence, not lose it. If the future is to develop in a way favorable to France, it is essential that she guard her freedom of action and initiative. For Europe to acquiesce in American control of its foreign and military policy would be, in de Gaulle's opinion, a sacrifice not only of its present dignity but of its long range interest. For America's interests and Europe's are not identical. Nations do differ: "when all is said and done, Great Britain is an island; France, the cape of a continent; America, another world." [111]

De Gaulle frequently refers to Yalta as the prime illustration of how little America can be relied on to guard or even understand Europe's problems and interests. Yalta was where the Anglo-Saxons and Russians presumed to "settle Europe's future in France's absence." [112] It has taken over twenty years, according to de Gaulle, for Europe even to begin to recover its balance after that ministration from without.[113] No doubt, de Gaulle found it not altogether inexpedient to be absent from Yalta. The "world would discover that there was a correlation between France's absence and new lacerations for Europe." [114]

Behind de Gaulle's fierce jealousy for independence is his fundamental assumption that the world is forever competitive and that no nation will survive that loses control of its own destiny. International differences are not a matter of evil intentions on either side. It is the nature of things in a competitive world that each nation will see to its own interests first and imagine that what is best for itself is also best for everyone generally. Mutually advantageous, and therefore durable international cooperation cannot be based on one nation's ceding the guardianship of its interests to another. Each nation must frankly assert its own interests, and then seek intelligently for a settlement which is genuinely to the benefit of all. That is, for de Gaulle, the true meaning of interdependence. Alliances are bargains between sharp bidders. A nation gets paid for the goods it can deliver. A nation without power fares badly from the charity of others. With such fundamental assumptions about international politics, it is understandable that de Gaulle has made every possible effort to give France the means for her own independent military defense.

France under de Gaulle—indeed, France under the Fourth Republic—has refused to renounce forever the means of independent defense and to accept total military dependence upon the United States.[115] She has made her own nuclear bombs without the illusion, de Gaulle has often said, that she was making herself the equal of America or that she no longer needed the American protective umbrella. Although the French deterrent was meant to have immediate effects, it was mostly important because it would preserve a measure of independence for the future:[116]

> It is obvious that one country, especially one such as ours, cannot in the present day and age and could not conduct a major modern war all by itself. To have allies goes without saying for us in the historic period we are in. But also for a great people to have the free disposition of itself and the means to struggle to preserve it is an absolute imperative, for alliances have no absolute virtues, whatever may be the sentiments on which they are based. And if one spontaneously loses, even for a while, the free disposition of oneself, there is a strong risk of never regaining it.[117]

> It is completely understandable that this French undertaking does not appear to be highly satisfactory to certain American circles. In politics and in strategy, as in the economy, monopoly quite naturally appears to the person who holds it to be the best possible system.[118]

France under de Gaulle has made great efforts to keep abreast of modern scientific research in all fields that might affect national power. Convinced that a nation must ultimately look to itself for the power to maintain its place in the world, de Gaulle is determined that France shall herself have the means to remain "in the front rank" of states. If he can prevent it, the melancholy fate foreseen by Roosevelt will never come to pass.

But if de Gaulle believes that competition and struggle are inevitable laws of life, he also believes that *mesure* is the essential characteristic of good leadership. France alone obviously lacks the resources to rival the United States or Russia. If she is to play a great role or even to retain her independence, she must have allies. And so de Gaulle has consistently sought help to balance against the "hegemonies" of the superpowers, including that of the United States within the noncommunist world.

The first major attempt at close alliance was with the British. All through the war, de Gaulle tried to win over Churchill to an Anglo-French combination as Europe's counterpoise to the superpowers on her periphery. Churchill paid a triumphal visit to liberated Paris in November, 1944, and de Gaulle, sensing that his British guests were impressed with exuberant French morale, thought it the moment to press forward with his already familiar theme of a close Franco-British partnership:

> You English, of course, will emerge from this war covered with glory. Yet to what a degree—unfair though it may be—your relative situation risks being diminished, given your losses and expenditures, by the centrifugal forces at work within the Commonwealth, and, particularly, the rise of America and Russia, not to mention China! Confronting a new world, then, our two old nations find themselves simultaneously weakened. If they remain divided as well, how much influence will either of them wield? [119]

De Gaulle was especially concerned with the settlement Roosevelt had in prospect for Europe.

> "The equilibrium of Europe," I added, "the guarantee of peace along the Rhine, the independence of the Vistula, Danube and Balkan states, the creation of some form of association with the

peoples all over the world to whom we have opened the doors of Western civilization, an organization of nations which will be something more than an arena for disputes between America and Russia, and lastly the primacy accorded in world politics to a certain conception of man despite the progressive mechanization of society—these, surely, are our great interests in tomorrow's world. Let us come to an agreement in order to uphold these interests together. If you are willing to do so, I am ready. Our two nations will follow us. America and Russia, hobbled by their rivalry, will not be able to raise any objection. Moreover, we shall have the support of many states and of world-wide public opinion, which instinctively shies away from giants. Thus England and France will together create peace, as twice in thirty years they have together confronted war.[120]

Churchill's answer was a more thoughtful version of what he had shouted at de Gaulle the preceding January at Marrakech: "How do you expect that the British should take a position separate from that of the United States? . . . each time we must choose between Europe and the open sea, we shall always choose the open sea. Each time I must choose between you and Roosevelt, I shall always choose Roosevelt." [121] In Paris, Churchill defended his policy by observing that:

. . . in politics as in strategy, it is better to persuade the stronger than to pit yourself against him. That is what I am trying to do. The Americans have immense resources. They do not always use them to the best advantage. I am trying to enlighten them, without forgetting, of course, to benefit my country. I have formed a close personal tie with Roosevelt. With him, I proceed by suggestion in order to influence matters in the right direction.[122]

De Gaulle's sour comment: "The peace we French hoped to build in accord with what we regarded as logic and justice, the British found it expedient to approach with formulas of empiricism and compromise." [123]

As far as de Gaulle was concerned, Churchill's reply marked the fundamental decision of postwar British policy. Britain had chosen America, not France; the Atlantic, not Europe.[124] While the French under de Gaulle have always been interested in military cooperation with England, the British have preferred an independent national force of their own. When that force seemed too expensive, they chose to depend on America rather than to throw in their lot with France.

That was what Nassau meant to de Gaulle. The British policy was nothing new. Macmillan was only following in the footsteps of Churchill. He was choosing the "deep blue sea." De Gaulle took his revenge over the Common Market. England was not European, he argued. It would be dangerous to admit a nation with so dubious an interest in forming a genuine European community.[125] But de Gaulle remains hopeful that the logic of events will someday lead the British to reconsider Churchill's choice.

Perhaps de Gaulle's most flamboyant diplomatic moves have been his periodic advances towards the communist world.[126] Soon after his unsuccessful campaign to interest Churchill in an Anglo-French alliance, de Gaulle took himself to Russia, there to see if "it would be possible to renew old Franco-Russian solidarity which, though repeatedly betrayed and repudiated, remained no less a part of the natural order of things, as much in relation to the German menace as to the endeavors of Anglo-American hegemony." [127] The result was the Franco-Russian Treaty of 1944 which allied the two countries against any German attack for the next twenty years. De Gaulle was only playing the old game of *equilibre*. Perhaps he underestimated the virulence of the future Russian threat to Western independence, but, according to his *Memoirs,* he had no illusions as to what Russian intentions were in Eastern Europe. Indeed, the treaty nearly remained unsigned because de Gaulle at Moscow refused to pay the price Stalin demanded. France refused to break off with the Polish government in London in favor of Stalin's puppet Lublin Committee.

Before long de Gaulle was completely disenchanted with the

communists, including the French variety who had cooperated in the Resistance and in the early days of the postwar government. It was clear that communists were loyal to Russia, not France.[128] His major political effort during the twelve years out of power, the Rassemblement du Peuple Français, appealed primarily to the need for a strong, progressive government to counter communism in and out of France.

Nevertheless, de Gaulle has always toyed with closer relations with Russia as a natural means for gaining France more independence and a better bargaining position with the American colossus. He fears Russia much less in the 1960's than formerly. Russia is now locked in a prolonged struggle with China in what some in France call the new Hundred Years' War. In the long run, de Gaulle may well believe, Russia cannot expect to hold her immense Eastern empire against the inexorable pressure of seven or eight hundred million Chinese. There is one last grand drama of decolonization yet to be played. The most tenacious of European colonizers, the Russians, will be forced to give in with the rest. In the distant future, a chastened and bourgeois Russia, cut down to a size that would make cooperation possible, may return of necessity to the European family. The Gaullist dream of Europe from the Atlantic to the Urals might become a reality and the old continent, rent asunder by revolution and civil war, would finally be restored as an independent entity between the Anglo-Saxons to the West and the new yellow colossus to the East.

It is unlikely that de Gaulle sees these combinations developing except in the distant future. For now, only tentative approaches Eastward can be made. Bridges can be built but not crossed. For the present at least, egged on by an expansionist ideology, bloated Russia remains a major threat to Europe—and the Atlantic Alliance a vital French commitment. Indeed, it is only because of the American defense of Europe that de Gaulle can dare move so close to the Russian bear. But however essential the Alliance, France must retain her freedom of action for the day when the next grand turning of events offers Europe the chance to escape from its present state of dependence and regain something like its old power.

The Third World of new states is another major area in which de Gaulle continues to seek support to bolster the independent position of France. It is only natural that he should exploit his position as an outsider to become the spokesman for all the nationalist forces in the world. The major requirement for this step, of course, was that France herself should cease to be a colonial power—perhaps the most dramatic achievement of de Gaulle's second reign.

Until he returned to power in 1958, de Gaulle was convinced that the French Union had to be preserved if France were to keep her status as a great power. He talked during those years of various federal schemes built around a strong French President, chosen in part by the Union. He was not unsympathetic to the more unselfish integrationist sentiments of *Algérie Française,* but events convinced him that nationalism was too strong a force to be contained within tight federal bonds. The attempt was exhausting France and poisoning her diplomatic relations. In a series of stunning tactical moves, de Gaulle gave up the Empire, including eventually Algeria.

Although de Gaulle gave up his original federalist dream, he has gone out of his way to maintain close relations with the former African colonies. The French continue to devote a higher proportion of their resources to foreign economic aid than any other major country.[129] They cannot, of course, match the enormous outlay of the United States. Nevertheless, what they spend is considerable and since their commitments are not universal, they can be more selective and perhaps use their resources with relatively greater political effect.[130]

Although her role in the Third World has given France new world-wide influence and prestige, it seems axiomatic to many that the greatest opportunity for increasing French power and independence lies in Europe. It cannot be said that de Gaulle has neglected Europe, or even that he has refused to cooperate with supranational Communities. Indeed, in certain respects, he has been the major force for economic integration.

After this necessarily selective and rapid survey of Gaullist principles, experiences, and policies, it should be possible to return to our original question: what is the basis of the Gaullist criticism of supranational Europe, and what is the grand alternative, the Europe of States, which de Gaulle would offer instead?

7.

De Gaulle's career has been too rich and too articulate to be summarized easily. His confederal approach to building a European union has been presented here as typically nationalist. To call him a nationalist is to say more than that he is an ardent lover of France. He is, of course, highly conscious of the priceless heritage of excellence and experience which lies in the great national cultures of Europe. He can be expected to resist the disappearance of those cultures into a mongrel culture of the lowest common denominator—a new Europe of ugly office buildings where everyone speaks "Volapuk." [131] He is for a *Europe des patries,* a Europe in which the separate national cultures do not disappear.

So are most people who are sensitive to the cultural heritage of the West. Nevertheless, as he himself points out, *la patrie* is one thing, *l'Etat* is another.[132] The former is sentimental and cultural, the latter has to do with responsible power and authority. Similarly, nationalism is not only an emotional attachment, but also a theory of the state. There is nothing in nationalist theory which ties a nationalist state forever to a single culture. The best theorists have always described the nation as an idea in men's minds. That idea can change.[133] Cultures which do not adapt lose their vitality and new nations can be created, voluntarily or otherwise. France was a creation of the monarchy. Britain was not formed by the spontaneous fusion of England, Scotland, Wales, and Ireland. What the nationalist emphasizes is not the fixity of nations, but the importance of a high degree of common identity if the state is to achieve a political consensus. Again, there is nothing in the theory of the national state which prevents its extension beyond the boundaries of the present national states if such an extension seems imperative for reasons of survival and there is sufficient shared identity to support a strong state.[134]

If de Gaulle's nationalist view has not made it absolutely impossible for him to consider the building of new states in the distant future, it has ensured that he would be sensitive to the difficulties of creating consensus where sufficient ties do not exist, and especially aware of the need for strong leadership to hold together and direct any diverse political community.

This basic nationalist view has had a number of effects on de Gaulle's European policy. Nationalism has determined many of the things he has opposed. He has sought to give the Community some definition by keeping out additional diverse elements, like England, and hoping to induce the Six to look more to each other and less to the United States. He has pushed for genuine economic integration, but opposed free trade. De Gaulle's nationalism has also led him to squelch consistently the plans and pretensions of the supranational Communities. Since they can never become a genuine state, he believes, their growth to sufficient power to enfeeble the national states would leave Europe without any effective government and thus an even easier target for outside intervention.

All these negative aspects of de Gaulle's European policy scarcely make him an enemy of European unity—except for those who believe that the Communities would become a European government if only de Gaulle would disappear, or for those who feel European unity is helped by American hegemony. For the rest, however, his negative policies would make him seem a tolerably good European were it not perhaps for a certain tone to Gaullist diplomacy and rhetoric which seems to arouse a not altogether reasonable antagonism in the federalist soul.

It is when de Gaulle turns to the positive side of his European policy, the Fouchet Plan, that his contribution is more ambivalent. The proposed confederacy is no less based on nationalist premises than his negative policies. Since de Gaulle believes there is no force in Europe strong enough to be a "federator," least of all the Brussels technocracy, a European union must proceed by a gradual harmonization of the political authorities of Europe, the states. It is to be hoped that through regular organized consultation, the states can bring their policies into harmony and be persuaded to act as a unit towards the outside world. Over a very long period of time, they and their citizens may even develop a sufficient identity with each other to merge into a common state. But any attempt to do so prematurely would only result in a feeble government.

The difficulty with this confederal approach is that its success depends on the possibility that Belgium, France, Germany, Holland, Italy, and Luxembourg can ever reach and maintain a basic agreement on their domestic and foreign policies.[135] Among the other difficulties of the Gaullist confederal scheme is that it would seem to contradict the basic principle of its own nationalist and Gaullist world view: that political consensus is nearly impossible to maintain among diverse interests, especially without institutions which provide for strong leadership to arouse a common identity.

Could a Gaullist believe that a coherent policy for Europe would ever be formulated from the six equal representatives of six separate states, each with its own particular interests to be achieved at the expense of the others? Assuming that de Gaulle is right and that the supranational Commission of the Common Market is indeed entirely unsuitable for the role of the Gaullist executive, where is the Gaullist leader in the Fouchet Plan? Where is the strong independent chief who meditates and resolves the ambitions of the parts into the higher interest of the whole? Who is the king to summon the wills of the people to the common good? If such arduous efforts of leadership are essential to maintaining consensus within a national community, why are they any less essential in a European community infinitely more diverse and without long habits of cooperation? If the Fourth Republic was a failure in France, why should it be a success in Europe? And why, above all, should de Gaulle be its advocate?

De Gaulle may have believed that his scheme was favored by special circumstances. If America and Britain were kept outside, France's resurgent diplomatic and military power and his own prestige and persuasiveness might have allowed him to dominate an assemblage of the six Continental states, including a highly vulnerable Germany. He must be sadly disillusioned. It was not even possible to agree on the institutions for discussing policy, let alone to reach any agreements on what that policy should be. The stormy career of the Franco-German Treaty has amply illustrated the weakness of voluntary confederations.

It is difficult, however, to see what other course towards union might have been taken by de Gaulle. He has no faith in the political future of technocracy. He finds it difficult to believe that any other national leader can take the Common Market seriously as a federal government. National leaders who advocate federation are, in his eyes, merely hiding their real lack of interest in any meaningful Continental unity. The lack of interest does not surprise him. He believes he knows why the Dutch have no desire to join closely with their larger neighbors. No one as conscious of history as de Gaulle can be surprised by the reluctance of the rest of Europe to accept him even as only a "confederator." De Gaulle's insuperable handicap as Europe's leader is that he so magnificently embodies its splendid past that he immediately arouses all its ancient hatreds and fears. Europe might come together around supermarkets and modern office buildings; it will never rally around Versailles.

There are no other federators on the scene, however. The

European federalists are even less likely to try a mass popular uprising than they would be to succeed at it. There are, on the other hand, strong forces working to keep the Six apart. The United States in recent years has suddenly renewed its interest in Atlantic integration and has intervened with considerable vigor to discourage too close Franco-German cooperation. Again de Gaulle is not surprised. He is more likely to despise the Germans for failing to see their own long-range interests or keep their nerve than to blame America for preferring a disunited and pliable Europe.

De Gaulle, after all, is not a utopian. He has tried federalism before and abandoned it when it failed. He has proposed what seemed to him the only conceivable solution for European unity, but he is probably not much interested in it anymore. Again, he has tried and failed.[136] Meanwhile, he has gone on building the position of France and exploiting all the possibilities for her prosperity and independence. He may still be looking for a satisfactory ally who can keep France in the front ranks, but not among the Six. There may be yet another act to the grand Gaullist drama.

The failure of the Fouchet Plan should offer little satisfaction to the partisans of Europe. De Gaulle did offer a genuine step towards unity. It could not have hurt Europe's cause to have regular organized consultation among the governments. It is difficult to see the European states accepting a common government until they have reached some consensus on foreign policy and defense. Nothing is gained by avoiding the attempt.

No doubt the present supranational institutions should not be sabotaged by any new political arrangements, but neither should it be forgotten that European bureaucrats are not altogether immune from the tendencies of bureaucrats elsewhere. They like power and fear change. It is not realistic to expect that the European administration can continue to grow without being subject to closer political control. Nor is it surprising that the Eurocrats should be reluctant to submit to that control. But

Europe can be built only by politicians, distasteful as they may be to the mandarins. In short, it was dangerous for the apparent friends of unity to go on delaying progress indefinitely. History goes by. To improve something, you must first have it. Once something is underway, its inadequacies can be reformed. The Articles of Confederation led to the Federal Constitution; the Fourth Republic did lead to the Fifth.

Above all, the partisans of Europe might well learn from de Gaulle a more profound view of the essential nature of a political community. Politics may not be quite so grim as de Gaulle believes; his monarchy may not be the government of the future, but surely his views have a sweep, a profundity, and above all, an allure that is almost entirely lacking among European and Atlantic federalists. If they are ever to realize their goals, if they are to have an intelligent effect upon the course of events, they would do well to study carefully not only de Gaulle but the whole body of nationalist political theory. The national state may have outlived its day. It nevertheless still remains the only political formula within which modern democratic societies have successfully organized themselves. The modern world did not begin in 1945. The insights of two centuries may still count for something.

V.

America's Atlantic Europe

V.

America's

Atlantic

Europe

Today's federalist generally looks forward to the integration not only of Europe but of the whole "Atlantic Community," meaning by that the United States, Western Europe, and Canada. This is the alternative that would build Europe around America. To match the Eurocrats there is an enthusiastic, powerful, and determined group of "Atlanticists." They share many federalist views with the Eurocrats, including, often, an enthusiasm for supranational European unity, and they flourish in much the same professional and governmental circles. Many are tied to France and the Eurocrats through Jean Monnet, and, like Monnet, some once had happy experiences working with the closely coordinated Anglo-American wartime bureaucracy.

Their ideal, Atlantic Union, has been current in advanced Western circles since before the last war. The present version envisages either close association between the European states and the American Union or an alliance of two equal partners—the United States of America and a United States of Europe. After World War II, America's power and Europe's need made some form of that union seem not only desirable but possible. America encouraged unity by introducing, along with its aid, those functionalist techniques of intergovernmental coordination that had been so successful in the wartime alliance with Britain. The foundation of postwar Atlantic unity has been the military alliance built around NATO and the American deterrent. The success of that alliance has led to the hope that it would endure and develop into a permanent Atlantic Confederation.

But America is another world, as de Gaulle and Churchill once observed—why should the United States remain permanently so involved in Europe's affairs? Why shouldn't America go home? How can there be enough consensus for a political community in so vast and diverse a region?

The essential premise of the Atlanticist would seem to be the old Hamiltonian argument that a larger community is more stable and can act more effectively in the outside world. Thus permanent American involvement in Europe is counted on to guard both against Europe's returning to the dangerous political instability of its prewar era and against America's lapsing into isolationism. It will provide a home for West Germany and a balance for Russia. An enormous market, moreover, is expected to ensure economic prosperity. Above all, an Atlantic Community would allow a rational sharing of the burdens of defense and foreign aid, and spare Europe the cost and danger of uncoordinated national atomic forces. Hence, the Atlanticist argues, any enlightened proposal for Europe's future must include Atlantic integration. Any scheme which threatens that integration is a dangerous and stupid retrogression towards nationalist instability.

All but the most sanguine Atlantic enthusiasts, however, agree that a democratic federal union between Europe and America is beyond any immediate hope. It is generally conceded that any community, particularly if it remains, as it must, heavily concerned with military matters, will have to be confederal in structure. For the present, the "Union" will remain voluntary and each member will reserve the right to dissociate itself from particular policies.[1]

Whatever Washington's announced plans for the future, up to the present time Atlantic unity has meant, in practical terms, that America leads and the others follow, sometimes reluctantly. America has been the indispensable leader, the federator essential to internal unity and external effectiveness. After the war, with Europe weak and demoralized, America became its supranational government in military matters. The President of Europe lived in Washington.

In theory, a confederation with one overwhelmingly preponderant power ought to have a better chance of holding together than a confederation of equals, though less opportunity for developing independent supranational institutions.

Whatever the theoretical prospects, the will of the Europeans to proceed towards a general Atlantic confederation is far from sure and enthusiasm for American leadership is far from universal. Some Europeans, in fact, see America not as a liberator and protector but as a jealous and petulent overlord. It has become fashionable in some circles to equate American hegemony with Russian, to talk of the liberation of the West as well as of the East. Gaullism is behind much of the criticism, but in this matter as in so many others, if de Gaulle did not exist he would probably have to be invented. His position corresponds to deep and enduring European attitudes and is bolstered by arguments concerning Europe's interest and security which cannot be brushed aside.

The foundation of Atlantic unity has been Europe's need for American military protection. But for several years a group of

French strategists and politicians has claimed that the American nuclear force is no longer a reliable safeguard for European defense.[2] Their arguments strike at the very heart of any Atlantic Union since the prospects for continuing, let alone intensifying, that Union depend upon the military alliance.

The American pledge to defend Europe was credible, the Gaullists argue, while the Western hemisphere was invulnerable, but the day is here when the Russians can inflict ruin and disaster on America itself. Many Europeans find it hard to believe that any American president would ever take the decision to stop a European invasion at so suicidal a cost.[3] Indeed, they were told as much by an American Secretary of State, Christian Herter, in 1958: "I can't conceive of the President involving us in an all-out nuclear war unless the facts showed clearly that we are in danger of devastation ourselves, or that actual moves had been made toward devastating ourselves."[4]

America's nuclear strategy in recent years, the celebrated counterforce doctrine, has only exacerbated Gaullist misgivings.[5] The old doctrine of massive retaliation assumed it was possible to draw a line around the vital interests of the West, from Germany to Matsu. If the enemy stepped beyond, the United States, from a position of relative invulnerability, would strike a massive retaliatory blow. American troops in Europe, for example, were merely tripwires to establish aggression and set off the deterrent.

The Kennedy administration, faced with the communists' new power to hit the United States itself and their increasing use of revolutionary subversion rather than direct military attack, concluded that massive retaliation was too violent and clumsy a strategic doctrine. Its new counterforce strategy called for a "selective response" which would confront an enemy, at each stage of an escalating conflict, with a punishment that made further aggression irrational. Even if nuclear weapons were finally used, they should be employed selectively.

Counterforce strategy called for precise control of all forces. The United States came to insist more and more on centralized control of Western military forces and was particularly opposed to the embryonic independent French deterrent. National deterrents, according to the Pentagon, were not only militarily ludicrous, but deplorable because they introduced unnecessarily complicating factors into a game of life and death requiring the most exact calculation and control.[6] Europeans were urged to fill out American nuclear power with conventional forces and thus increase the "options" open to Western defense.

The Gaullists have seized upon the new strategy as clear evidence that Europe can no longer rely entirely on America for protection. The basic tenet of their argument has been that effective European defense can only be nuclear. While a nuclear war would be fatal for Europe, they argue, another massive conventional war would be scarcely less undesirable. In any event, the object of all strategy for Europe is not to punish but to prevent aggression. Nuclear weapons, for all their immense destructiveness, have one great advantage: they make aggression too costly ever to be rational. The only real danger of war in Europe, the argument runs, will come when the enemy is tempted to believe that his aggression will not be punished by nuclear retaliation. Anything which reduces the credibility of a nuclear deterrent enhances the prospect of war. That is precisely the effect, the Gaullists maintain, of American nuclear strategy with its emphasis on conventional forces and selective response.[7]

The new American strategy, the Gaullists argue, is compatible with America's interests, but not with Europe's. It is understandable that a nation, no matter how close its friendship with others, will not get involved in full-scale nuclear war for anything except its own survival. In some future crisis the Russians may be tempted to test America's unlikely commitment. Hence, Europe remains in greater danger of war until there is a deterrent in Europe itself. The argument is convincing to many Europeans and indeed to many of the best American students of nuclear strategy.[8] Its obvious conclusion is that Europe cannot entrust its defense to a Western alliance in which America is not only the leader, but the only real nuclear power.

The real question behind the argument is whether the Atlantic is enough of a community to have an integrated defense. Will America's interests, now and forever, be that close to those of Europe? The Gaullist position embodies the essential nationalist argument against all federalist communities: a federation lacks the consensus to become a state; it undermines states, but it cannot replace them. Unfortunately, a confederation built around a nuclear military alliance raises at the very outset the question of consensus in its ultimate and most difficult form: is there a sufficient harmony of interest and identity among the members so that in an extreme emergency they will all risk annihilation together? The American states take this unity for granted among themselves. California will die for New York. Is the Atlantic such a community? The Gaullists would prefer not to bet their survival that it is. America will not destroy itself for Europe, they believe. Europe does not want itself destroyed for America. France builds its own nuclear force undeterred by American disapproval.

Probably the majority of Europeans disagree. They not only fear the spread of nuclear weapons but doubt the present and future efficacy of a national or even a European deterrent. Thus they fear losing American protection more than they do any hypothetical Russian gamble on American intentions. But even those European Atlanticists who defend most fiercely the need for an integrated Western defense under a single command, and who concede that the command must be American, nevertheless vehemently insist that there must be joint consultation and planning far beyond anything yet seen in NATO. It is too much to expect the Europeans both to renounce independent action and to remain in the dark about America's strategic plans for their defense.[9]

While the President of Europe lives in Washington, the Europeans do not elect him and have little to say about his actions in those sudden crises which, because of the Alliance, involve Europe's fate as well as America's. America has too often gone to the brink over disputes outside Europe without asking its interdependent allies if it were a journey they cared to make. The spread of Gaullist resentment in Europe can be contained, the Atlanticists believe, only by making the Alliance more federal, by creating those institutions and practices that will nourish mutual trust and common identity between Europe and its American leader. In short, if the Atlantic Alliance is to last, America's leadership must be. less imperial and more federal.

America's enthusiasm for sharing strategic decisions, however, has been tepid. De Gaulle has made several fruitless suggestions for a directorate of Atlantic great powers.[10] Both Britain and France have felt impelled to acquire a separate deterrent, not only to be independent but to force their way into American strategic planning.[11] If Gaullism be defined abstractly as the desire of a nation to preserve its freedom of action, Gaullism has long flourished not only in London but above all in Washington. The American planning process, it is said, does not easily lend itself to formal foreign participation.[12] The major difficulty is that military problems are seldom purely technical but involve ultimately the whole range of foreign policy, not only in the North Atlantic but in the world at large. Yet the broader the scope of the issues discussed, the less likely is any advance agreement on policy. It is doubtful if disunity in the Alliance is merely the result of faulty institutions for consultation. What kind of policy would have emerged in Cuba or Vietnam if America had waited for the approval of the European allies?

The Gaullist does not so much blame America for its independence as remain unconvinced that France and Europe have necessarily the same interests as the United States. In short, he refuses to believe that they can ever become a permanent, closely integrated Atlantic Community. Europe cannot go on having its vital decisions made in America and there is not enough common interest for the decisions to be made together.

The American government has long professed to realize that the present exclusiveness of its control would have to be modified to accommodate Europe's reviving political will. American policy has been to support Europe's revival and its drive towards political federation. Europe was to be an "equal partner" to share the burdens of world leadership. The assumptions behind this "dumbbell" theory have apparently been that partnership would be possible only with a united Europe and that a supranational federation growing out of the Common Market was the only desirable form of European union.[13]

The American government has made two major proposals for the Alliance: President Kennedy's "Grand Design," and the Multilateral Nuclear Force.[14]

The Grand Design called for a partnership between America and a federal Europe strengthened and leavened by the addition of Britain. The two halves or "pillars" were to be bound more closely by the "Kennedy Round" of tariff cuts, the beginning possibly of an Atlantic free-trade area. The whole proposal was admirably suited to reconcile European federalists to Atlantic Union.[15] But, for the usual reason, General de Gaulle saw the Grand Design as only a subtle blueprint for continuing American hegemony indefinitely, America's ingenious device for drowning Gaullist France in an incoherent European federation.

The second proposal, the MLF, would have created a joint Atlantic nuclear force with mixed crews, subject to a veto by each of the participants. On the whole it was welcomed by European Atlanticists who felt it gave promise of genuine consultation on nuclear strategy. The Gaullists, however, felt the scheme not only thwarted their aspirations but insulted their intelligence. In addition to the General's well-known distaste for mixed crews, the Gaullists and their friends were not interested in a finger on the trigger of some force ultimately subject to an American veto; they wanted a trigger of their own. America, they observed, was keeping the bulk of its own nuclear force outside the MLF. The American force had only one trigger, in Washington. In short, MLF changed nothing. The Alliance meant Europeans sacrificed their independence, while America did not.

De Gaulle's violent reaction against the MLF and his veto of England's joining the Common Market frustrated American plans for strengthening the Atlantic Community. In turn, the United States blocked the Gaullist design for Europe by attacking it at its very foundation, the Franco-German entente. The Germans were told that de Gaulle's Europe was not America's Europe.[16] America wanted unity, but not de Gaulle's "inward-looking" Europe of States. Since Erhard's German government shared little of Adenauer's enthusiasm for de Gaulle and preferred, not unreasonably, the American deterrent to the French, any effective Franco-German partnership to build Europe ceased. Whether it is in America's long-range interest to frustrate de Gaulle by becoming more closely tied to Germany is another matter. It will not, presumably, make a settlement with Russia any easier.[17] At any rate, the United States and France together have now blocked the unity of Europe. Each insists on its own version of unity or no union at all. Since they have frustrated each other, each has leaned towards what seem extreme but complementary nationalist positions. America would renounce partnership; France, the Alliance.

A number of influential Americans now argue that American interest requires Europe to remain divided and American supremacy in the Alliance to continue. The United States can be quietly grateful to de Gaulle for preventing federal unity. The arrangement of Western power into two equal blocs might easily lead to a dangerous economic and political rivalry. It would in no way advance world stability. It would only complicate our ever reaching the fundamental entente with the Russians that might bring real stability to the postwar world. The disunited states of Europe must realize that America is a great power and they are not, that America will continue to keep control of the vital decisions which affect her own survival and will not take kindly to any European attempt to set up a rival Western great power, an "inward-looking" Continental bloc without her close ally, Britain. Some Europeans may find this harsh, but nothing can come from misplaced sentimentality which obscures the facts of life. Europe depends on the United States; the United States does not depend on Europe. In the rather uncharacteristic words of Walter Lippmann:

> The President is quite right in telling the French and the Germans that while the United States has no intention of withdrawing from Europe, Europe must realize that the United States could be pushed out of Europe. It could be pushed out if we were maneuvered into a position where we had to defend Europe while the critical decisions that led to war were to be made not in Washington but in Paris or Bonn.[18]
>
> We are at odds with him [de Gaulle] because in fact his ambition to take the leadership of Europe is irreconcilable with our vital need to retain the ultimate power in nuclear affairs. We must have that power because we have the ultimate responsibility.[19]
>
> We do not have a divine right to have in our own hands, rather than in European hands, the ultimate decisions. But it is in our interest to hold on to the ultimate decisions, if we can, and we must not be beguiled and bemused by any sentimental adulation of venerable statesmen who are not moved by sentimentality. In other words, we shall have to play the game and be resourceful enough to protect our ultimate interest and to promote our bigger hopes.[20]

But the American "Gaullist" argument has its European counterpart which asserts that the day is soon coming when, for Europe, the Atlantic Alliance will be an impediment instead of a necessity. To begin with, the Gaullists argue, the American bluff can be called. In the short run America is not likely to permit a conquest of Europe, no matter how disenchanted she becomes with European governments.[21] In the long run, of course, American vulnerability will make its deterrent unreliable, but the French deterrent will eventually become a force that cannot be ignored. Most important of all, a Russian invasion is rapidly ceasing to be possible. Russia is far too embroiled with China to attempt any such ambitious expansion towards the West. Europe, therefore, has no compelling need to remain in America's military confederation and in fact has far more to gain from ties to Russia. After all, Russia is a European power. She is much weaker than

America and hence would be a more satisfactory ally. Furthermore, her immense undeveloped consumers' market and advanced technological skill offer Western European industry the resources it needs to catch up with the industrial giants across the Atlantic and thus stop Europe's colonization by American industry. Finally, only Russia can settle the German question.

Behind the Gaullist argument is the belief that America has grown too powerful, that the balance of power has tilted too much in her favor for the health of the rest of the world. Equilibrium can be restored only by a Europe extending from the Atlantic to the Urals. That is the only way that the Europeans can keep from becoming permanent American economic and military satellites. They do not seem to fear Russian hegemony. A Russia which can no longer control Poland or Rumania will not, they reckon, be in a position to dominate France.

At all costs, the Gaullists feel, Europe must prevent another Yalta, another grand settlement between Russia and the Anglo-Saxons over the heads of Europeans—perhaps in the form of a sweeping disarmament treaty by which the two embattled superpowers move to recapture and freeze forever the bipolar world of the postwar era.

To prevent a pact between Russia and America, Europe must reject American leadership and move closer to Russia. Europeans who toy with these views suspect both America and Russia of sharing a certain nostalgia for the Cold War. Both countries, they argue, have a taste for ideological oversimplification. Both prefer a black and white world where they are the unchallenged leaders of the good. They are uncomfortable in the present plural world which they find too sophisticated and too complicated. Moreover, the habit of command is difficult to give up. But, in the eyes of such Gaullists, true progress towards a stable and normal world lies in breaking down the old hegemonies so that no one is too powerful and every nation can have reasonable elbowroom to work out its own destiny.

Both the extreme Gaullist and the extreme American positions are to some extent daydreams, imaginary escapes from the frustrating necessities that demand an Atlantic Alliance. In the long run, of course, it might be expected that the United States would grow weary of its involvements and that Europe would move towards normal relations with Russia. But unless forced by American intransigence in Europe or belligerence in the rest of the world, neither Europe nor France is likely to make a drastic switch in alignment or even move towards neutralism. The ties of the Atlantic Community are reinforced by too much interest, sentiment, and habit.[22]

For a great many in Europe, Gaullism, despite its appeal, requires too much effort and too much risk. In the smaller countries especially, there is no shortage of Europeans who would prefer to relax in their golden chains and leave the management of the world to America. They would prefer American hegemony to the leadership of any European power. They see no real hope for a genuine European unity. Nationalism, they believe, has again proved too strong among the exquisitely individualistic countries of the old continent. The postwar moment of common weakness and fresh ideas, when a unified Europe might have been created, has passed. Since Europeans prefer America to each other, only the United States can bring order into the coalition. Without the Atlantic tie, Europe would be in chaos and an easy prey for a less kindly master. The United States is Europe's supranational government. There can never be another—except the Russians.

Others in Europe, while not necessarily despairing of European unity, nevertheless deplore the old-fashioned power politics of the Gaullists as a far too dangerous game for the modern atomic world. Fear of nuclear war dwarfs any nostalgia for independent national power. Europeans must give up having grand policies of their own. The West must remain together and fate has made America its leader. As Europe grows in economic power, her influence will inevitably weigh more heavily in Washington. Time and patience will bring a gradual evolution of federal institutions. These Europeans follow Churchill rather than Machiavelli; they prefer to ally with the strong rather than with the weak.

These fundamental attitudes, strongly rooted in public opinion and government, would seem to ensure that the Atlantic Community, not as any particular structure but as the close alliance between Europe and America, has a not unpromising future as long as nothing disturbs the normal trend of relations. At first, that was the reaction of most Atlanticists to de Gaulle's attacks on the Alliance. Atlanticists planned to ride out the Gaullist storm, waiting until the old man should have died, that France might reverently subside. But as Europe and the West have appeared to grow more and more disunited, the Atlanticists have grown frightened of de Gaulle and their bitterness against him knows few bounds. To them, he is only a new Mussolini, pursuing the same tawdry dreams of national grandeur. Nevertheless, they find him a great danger and there appears to be a new hardness in the federalist camp, a determination to use power as skillfully and, if need be, as bluntly as de Gaulle himself uses it. Many Atlanticists now believe it would be shortsighted and cowardly not to use all the effective power available against the increasingly ruthless attack of the arch-disintegrator.

The partisans of Atlantic unity are not without formidable resources. They appeal to an influential section of public opinion. They occupy key positions in many governments and in the European Communities. Above all they have hopes of enlisting the immense power of the American government. By forcing such proposals for integration as the MLF, they believe the United States could create institutions that would start a genuine federalizing process in the Atlantic Alliance and thus begin eroding the stubborn nationalist centers of power that resist both American leadership and European federal integration. The pressure brought to bear over MLF called sharp attention to the degree to which America has penetrated Europe.

American power is colossal and its machinery has expanded

relentlessly. The American bureaucracy, like all others, tends to build empires. There is now a gigantic establishment of Americans concerned with foreign affairs. In every capital there are invariably several large contingents of American diplomats and experts. A considerable number of able American officials occupy themselves with NATO. An impressive portion of the American intellectual community is caught up in the study and practice of international politics. To be sure, this great establishment marks a mature acceptance of the great burden which fate has thrust upon the new world leader. It must be admitted, however, that if the burdens of world power were accepted reluctantly by the last generation, the present one has come to enjoy them thoroughly.

Power, of course, cannot be avoided and America inevitably has a great role to play. Nevertheless, it should not be overlooked that much of America's success as a leader has come from the widespread conviction that Americans can be trusted with power where others cannot. To note these feelings is not necessarily to be sentimental, but only to recognize realistically what has been, in fact, a major source of real American authority. Before allowing her power to be enlisted to impose an ideal on others, America had better give that ideal a close look to see whether it corresponds to her real interests, whether it cannot be achieved in some other way, and whether it appeals to her better or worse instincts.

A strong federalist bias has inspired the major American proposals for the Alliance. The MLF calls for the integration of military forces, down to the level of mixed crews. The Grand Design demands supranational European unity built around the Common Market. To begin with, both proposals have the not inconsiderable disadvantage of being unacceptable to the major power on the Continent. It is also questionable, in both instances, whether so federalist an approach is in America's own interest. Several books have been written discussing whether Atlantic integration, as envisaged in the MLF, will help or hinder the United States in arriving at a basic settlement with Russia.[23]

Certainly too great a commitment to West Germany does not lend flexibility to the American position. It is just possible, of course, that de Gaulle may prove in the end to be the indispensable mediator. A tighter unity might well increase disagreement over problems in the Third World.

It is even more questionable whether insistence on only a federal variety of European unity is in America's national interest or even relevant to it.[24] Is it really true that she can accept only equals as partners or that it will be easier to deal with a federal than a confederal Europe? Would England ever join the federal Europe envisaged by the United States?

The value to American interests of federalist integration is sufficiently dubious to call into question that dedication to federalist solutions which has ensured French opposition to all United States proposals for reforming the Atlantic Alliance. Should even more American power and prestige be put behind such proposals? Why is the federalist approach so precious to Washington?

There is much in the federalist ideal that is typical of our American culture. The belief that nations can be tied together by tables of organization probably appeals to something fundamental in every American. After the First World War, Irving Babbitt wrote that if an American is told the world is in danger, his first instinct is to set up a committee.[25] If Babbitt were alive today, he would doubtless be bemused by the rather fantastic proliferation of those pacts, councils, and study groups by which America has sought to coordinate the world. Babbitt might decide that America's campaign to build a new world order was merely the latest expression of its ancient Puritan tradition of vigorously improving other people's affairs. The American Puritan conscience, Babbitt knew, is a terrible and lawless force when aroused. Fortunately for domestic tranquillity, after this war it turned on communism rather than alcohol. But world government is perhaps only "social engineering" on a bigger scale.

In pursuing an examination of conscience, Americans might do well to consider de Gaulle's judgment of Roosevelt's "American Century." Behind the noble-sounding aims, de Gaulle found only the will to power, cloaked in idealism. But not even de Gaulle believed Roosevelt was an evil man. What lay between de Gaulle on one side and Roosevelt, the one-worlders, and the Atlanticists on the other was a profoundly different view of international politics. Roosevelt, like Wilson before him, hoped to capture the wild forces of international politics and enclose them within a structure where they could be bridled by reason and law. The assumption was that intergovernmental organizations could bring the same security to the international world as the state had brought to the domestic. Power would be brought under law. Peace was mostly a problem of organization.

As de Gaulle sees the international arena, it will always know competition, danger, and adventure. Power politics are not disease but life. Every generation has new challenges and must play its game. Those who play with style delight history and sometimes leave the world a better place. At worst, they preserve the independence and unity of their peoples. But for de Gaulle there are never final solutions. Tidy international systems which are supposed to control all conflict are invariably devices for imposing hegemony on others, for smothering the vitality of rising peoples in the endless seesawing of power which is the world.

De Gaulle speaks from a continent which has known many wars and little unity; Roosevelt, from a vast federation whose unruly forces have been kept in union, even if sometimes by force. For Roosevelt, federal world organization was the program of Washington and Hamilton, for de Gaulle it is that of Metternich. Those on top are always on the side of law and order:

> Playing Metternich is not a happy role . . . who . . . would have guessed that America, of all countries, would one day cast herself for Metternich's dreary part.[26]

Dreary or not, America is a conservative nation, the leader of the rich in a hungry world. Such a world probably needs enlightened conservatism more than revolutionary fervor. Europe, too, is rich and conservative. Probably nothing but their own boredom could lead the Europeans to start a war. It is difficult to imagine even a virulently Gaullist Europe with interests and aims far different from America's.[27] When de Gaulle has cured France of her inferiority complex, when the Gaullists have proved to themselves that they are independent, they are very likely to return to the idea of European integration and Atlantic partnership.

The French, once having got a genuine deterrent, will not be eager to see that the Germans have one as well. And if the Europeans move towards a reasonable settlement with Russia, how could the resulting stability harm American interests? If the German question can be solved, it will eliminate the major territorial stumbling block to an American rapprochement with Russia. If within a community of fundamental common interest Europe is a powerful and agile rival, what is there to fear? Americans are not afraid of competition; our diplomats have no monopoly on solving the problems of Africa, Asia, and South America. The difference in outlook between the United States and a self-confident Europe would enrich both.[28] It is not as if the quality of our American civilization leaves us without challenges at home.

In short, close relations between America and Europe seem probable in the natural course of events. It would be a pity if future cooperation were complicated by heavy-handed efforts to force it into some particular institutional formula that appeals to the American penchant for elaborate international machinery. America must stop taking sides on what form of unity is best for the Europeans. She must stop throwing her weight around in Europe.

It is all too human for a mature America to rejoice in its splendid power. But power is only an abstraction, even if it can be measured in computers. It would be too bad to lose sight of the difference between influencing friends and coercing enemies.

Coercion used on friends may compel obedience, but it also destroys friendship and trust. It would be ironical but sad if America were to adopt the brutal style of Gaullist diplomacy. De Gaulle, for all his brilliant insight, has never succeeded in having allies who were also friends. The Atlantic will be a community, not an empire. If America wants Europe to be a partner, she must let it be itself and not what she chooses to make it.

VI.

Nobody's Europe?

VI.
Nobody's
Europe?

If America cannot force unity on Europe, can Europe unify itself? It used to be taken for granted that some form of European union was both necessary and probable. In a world of super-powers, federalism was thought to be Europe's only hope for independence. But nationalism has revived with such vigor that the present often appears to be not an age of federalism but an age of nationalism—not a period of concentration, but a period of disintegration. True, there are many new international organizations filling vital common needs, but no federalizing center has eclipsed the nationalist state as the source of political power and democratic legitimacy. The step between international cooperation and federalism remains a conscious choice rather than a surreptitious process. In Europe, the Common Market has not set to work a hidden logic that guarantees union.

Meanwhile, the world grows less rather than more unified. The blocs are disintegrating, and the retreat of empires from Asia and Africa has extended the nation-state to every corner of the globe.

The strategy of nuclear defense, once thought to freeze the world into two great concentrations, seems instead to be having an opposite effect. Since each of the superpowers can now destroy the other, their mutual strength has become a common weakness. In the "balance of terror," neither dares use its enormous force. In the "phantom world" that results, a state like France can exercise a great influence with economic blandishments and cultural prestige.[1] True, Gaullist grandeur exists only in the shadow world, but no one wants to venture to the real world and nuclear war, not even for the pleasure of humbling de Gaulle.

In the long run, moreover, nuclear weapons may well lead to a greater fragmentation of world power than has hitherto existed in this century. Advocates of national deterrents suggest that eventually any modern industrial nation will be capable of an impregnable nuclear striking force, and that it will never be rational for any power, no matter how superior, to attack a country which, even if annihilated at one blow, can still wreak tremendous devastation on its attacker. A revolution in military technology may well have made defense inpregnable against offense. If true, smaller countries will have achieved a relative equality undreamed of in the era of massive armies, navies, and air forces.

As a result, it can be argued that the proliferation of nuclear weapons would increase world stability. No one would dare attack anyone else. Terror would be a powerful incentive to interdependence. Each nation would be impelled by its own self-interest to make sure that no country's misfortunes ever drove it to desperation. Nuclear weapons have given, in short, an unexpected revival to the old and once discredited nationalist principle that world peace and national independence are complementary. It is possible to foresee a revival of the Wilsonian argument of national self-determination: that national states can be expected to coexist harmoniously while the chief threat to peace will come from those modern Austria-Hungarys that hope to extend a state beyond the normal bounds of national consensus. In a nuclear world, it may be argued, civil strife in an ungainly federal state is more likely than a war between nations. Thus nationalism threatens to rob federalism of yet another of its chief supports, the claim to be the only principle around which a stable world order can be organized. As a result of the surprising revival of nationalism, the comfortable expectations of federalism have been disappointed. It appears that the ultimate unity of Europe is not inevitable; it is perhaps not even likely.

In history there are few things which are inevitable, and there is generally a great role open to determined men with clear ideas of what they want and how to get it. De Gaulle has always owed much of his power to knowing what he wants. His Europeanist opponents are so divided among themselves and so attached to particular unrealistic formulas that they often seem incapable of little beyond intransigent and increasingly ill-tempered opposition. They block de Gaulle's unity, but they offer nothing truly creative which might transcend the divisions between Gaullist nationalism and supranational federalism. Meanwhile, Europe remains disunited.

Ideals are the tools by which men seek to direct history. If events in Europe are out of control at present, it is to a considerable extent the fault of the ideals that each group has proposed. This book has been a study of those alternative ideals. Its primary object has been to explain each scheme along with the assumptions and values of its proposers. Its presupposition has been that only by understanding each alternative fully will it be possible to make a rational choice of the best from each. None of the alternatives has been found to be without wisdom, grandeur, and noble aspiration. But each has its own internal contradictions and practical weaknesses. Each, in short, is an inadequate ideal. Neither federalism nor nationalism is in itself a full enough theory to comprehend the realities and needs of modern political life.

What is needed is a modern theory of political community

which combines the fundamental nationalist insight into the problem of democratic consensus and leadership with the functionalist appreciation for the possibilities of bureaucratic planning and management on an international scale. And if nationalism and federalism are not to meet in their common extreme, the totalitarian and imperialist police-state, both need somehow to be imbued with the Personalist concern for the conditions which determine life for the average individual. Those who would unify Europe need to realize that in any European Community political consensus will be extremely difficult to maintain; that a federal Europe will have most of the problems of the present national states and many more; that it will, of necessity, have to turn towards those institutions that provide leadership and create consensus within the nation. If America, France, and even Britain need a "presidential" system, so will Europe. When good Europeans begin thinking along these lines, when they transcend rather than merely reject nationalism, then they may come to direct history rather than lament its course.

Since politics is the art of the possible and ideals must live with facts, it may be fitting to conclude with some obvious but often disregarded limitations on any practical idea for European unity. De Gaulle's France is the first fact that must be accepted. In spite of his concrete contributions to economic integration, it has been all too easy to blame the failure of unity on de Gaulle. But even if he were to disappear tomorrow, the issues he has exposed would remain as would the essential inadequacy of the supranational approach. Furthermore, a great many students of French politics who deplore Gaullism admit that his foreign policy corresponds to the fundamental wishes of most Frenchmen.

In foreign policy, France without de Gaulle would probably still be Gaullist.[2] France is a major power. Her capacity for causing trouble is great. If driven into angry isolation she might well turn to close relations with Russia, in which case NATO would become unworkable and Germany's position intolerable. A European Union, even of a Gaullist variety, would tie France to her neighbors and presumably would moderate her policies towards Russia and the United States. Moderation would be the price of leadership. De Gaulle's Europe of States may well be the only way to save the Alliance. Those who have opposed the Fouchet Plan in the name of Atlantic unity have been working against their own cause.

Secondly, it should be recognized that a supranational federal state built from the Common Market is an impossibility as long as it is opposed by both France and Britain, two of the three major European powers. Holland may be willing to give up her independence to Brussels, though that is doubtful, but France and Britain are not. Were the British in the Common Market, they would doubtless become even more opposed to supranationalism than the French. No one sincerely interested in unity should oppose the Europe of States in the name of federalism. There will be either a Europe of States or no unity at all.[3]

Thirdly, it should be recognized that a unified Europe cannot be formed without Britain. The French have tried to build Europe around a German alliance and have failed. Germany is too vulnerable and her interest too uncertain to be a reliable ally. De Gaulle conjures up too many divisive memories of the past ever to lead Europe by himself. Is it conceivable that Holland, which for centuries has defined itself in opposition to whatever great autocratic Catholic power was hoping to dominate Europe, would ever accept a Union of States in which de Gaulle clearly dominated? Events have made clear that the answer is no. Only Anglican England might reconcile Catholic and Protestant Europe to each other. Probably only an imperial nation of shopkeepers could harmonize the aspirations of those Continentals who are interested in power with those who are interested in trade. Only British banking and technology might make Europe's economy the equal of America's. Only its firmest ally could reconcile the United States to a new Western superpower.

But if England would lead Europe, she must join it. The one indispensable condition for European union is a close alliance between Britain and France. For Britain, it means going back on Churchill's alliance with the strong. It means accepting the Gaullist vision of a Europe that looks to itself first and is genuinely independent of America. It means the end of the "special relation" with America. It means gambling on greatness and the end, no doubt, of a certain comfortable detachment.

But the British have always been an adventurous people. Theirs has been an open and adaptable culture. They are used to playing a great role in the world. The quiet acceptance of decline, however admirably mature, is probably not the best solution either for them or for the rest of the world. It is certainly not the best solution for Europe.

Notes

I. EUROPE'S FUTURE, THE BATTLE OF IDEALS

1. Alexander Hamilton, "The Federalist, No. 1," in *The Federalist* (New York, The Modern Library), p. 3.

II. NATIONALISM VS. FEDERALISM IN POSTWAR EUROPE

1. See Bernard Voyenne, *Histoire de l'Idée Européenne*, and René Albrecht-Carrié, *One Europe.*

2. I develop this argument in a recent book on the nationalist theory of the English poet and philosopher, S. T. Coleridge, *Coleridge and the Idea of the Modern State* (New Haven, 1966).

3. The definition of the normally so judicious Henri Brugmans, *Panorama de la Pensée Fédéraliste*, p. 51. A more balanced view is found in Hannah Arendt, *The Origins of Totalitarianism* (Cleveland, 1958). The classic definition probably remains Ernest Renan, *Qu'est-ce qu'une nation?* (Paris, 1882).

4. Standard histories of nationalism are Carlton J. H. Hayes, *The Historical Evolution of Modern Nationalism* (New York, 1931), and Hans Kohn, *Nationalism: Its History and Meaning* (Princeton, 1955).

5. See Bernard Bosanquet, *The Philosophical Theory of the State* (London, 1910).

6. Disraeli's political novels written in the middle of the last century provide a fascinating discussion of the modern relationships of monarchy, democracy, and aristocracy. See *Coningsby, Sibyl*, and especially, *Tancred*.

7. Mazzini and Woodrow Wilson are two obvious examples.

8. The conservative nationalism of Burke, hoping to preserve traditional national culture and institutions, was a far more genuine nationalism, it can certainly be argued, than the imperialism of the French Revolution which sought to impose a universal formula on all peoples.

9. Tocqueville's preoccupation with centralism comes immediately to mind. France probably produced the greatest federalist of the last century in Pierre-Joseph Proudhon, and of this century in Emmanuel Mounier.

10. See, for example, S. T. Coleridge, "The Friend," *Works*, Shedd, ed. Vol. 2, First Section, Essays 10, 13, and 14. Mazzini, following Herder, assumed an automatic international harmony once each nation was independent.

11. See, for example, Sidney Webb in Fabian Essays (1889).

12. For the essential argument, see Bernard Bosanquet, *Social and Political Ideals: Being Studies in Patriotism* (London, 1917).

13. Racism and nationalism are, of course, completely different and, indeed, opposed. Nationalism seeks to achieve psychological unity among diverse classes. Racism has traditionally been the doctrine of a group in society claiming permanent superiority over the others. See, for example, Joseph-Arthur de Gobineau, *Essay on the Inequality of the Human Races* (Paris, 1853–55). Totalitarianism, according to Hannah Arendt, follows a policy of "rootlessness and neglect of national interests rather than nationalism." *Origins of Totalitarianism*, p. 417.

14. Carl J. Friedrich, "New Tendencies in Federal Theory and Practice," General Report, 6th World Congress. IPSA, Sept., 64, p. 3.

15. See Voyenne, *Histoire*, and its bibliography. For studies of pluralist thought, see the writings of such scholars as John N. Figgis, Frederic Maitland, and Otto von Gierke.

16. A good survey of modern European federalist movements and ideas, from which I have learned a great deal and which I have followed closely here, is Henri Brugmans, *L'Idée Européenne, 1918–1965*. Its author is Rector of the College of Europe in Bruges and among the most distinguished contemporary federalist theorists. I am grateful to him for his kind patience with a recalcitrant nationalist.

17. Perhaps the chief philosopher of the movement was Emmanuel Mounier who also directed the review, *Esprit*. Others included Robert Aron, Karl Barth, Jacques Maritain, Alexandre Marc and Denis de Rougement. Personalists began another important review, *L'Ordre Nouveau*.

18. Clarence Streit, *Union Now* (London, 1939).

19. De Gaulle, in London as Premier Reynaud's representative, thought the offer a splendid gesture. Monnet, doubtless, took it more seriously. See de Gaulle, *Call to Honor*, p. 74.

20. Altiero Spinelli places great importance on the enthusiasm of the Resistance throughout Europe for federal unity. It was significant in Italy, as he himself illustrates. In France, although Michel's standard history claims a great interest in federalism, the main emphasis, like that of Gaullism in general, seems to have been national renewal. See Henri Michel, *Les Courants de Pensée de la Résistance*. My judgment is strengthened after a conversation with Robert Salmon, once a prominent Resistance writer. A fascinating account of Salmon's group is Marie Granet, *Défense de la France*.

21. Brugmans, *L'Idée Européenne*, pp. 99 ff.

22. *Ibid.,* pp. 107 ff.

23. I owe this and many other interesting observations to Altiero Spinelli. His trenchant style has long refreshed students weary of fuzzy-minded cant.

24. J. J. Rousseau, "A Discourse on the Origin of Inequality," in *The Social Contract and Discourses,* G. D. H. Cole, ed. (New York: Dutton, 1950), p. 275.

25. There is, of course, nothing inconsistent in a nation-state with a federal constitution. The United States and Germany are federal. There is a certain confusing tendency among federalist writers to assume that only federalists can be constitutionalists who believe in the separation and dispersion of power. Many nationalist writers, of course, were constitutionalists. Indeed, as I argue in my book on Coleridge (see note 2), nationalism is probably essential to the constitutional state.

26. Alexander Hamilton, "The Federalist No. 9," in *The Federalist* (New York, The Modern Library), p. 49.

27. Brugmans, *Panorama,* Chap. 16.

28. *Ibid.,* Chap. 17.

29. For an exhaustive discussion of the phenomenon by many students, see Léo Hamon and Albert Mabileau, *La Personnalisation du Pouvoir.*

30. De Gaulle, Press Conference, Algiers, April 21, 1944; *Unity, Documents,* p. 327.

31. De Gaulle himself warmly praised the American initiative as "clairvoyante" because it engaged Europe in solidarity. Speech before the Anglo-American Association of Paris, July 9, 1947 (micro.).

32. Ronald Steel, *The End of Alliance: America and the Future of Europe.*

33. Populations and Areas (*The Americana Annual,* 1935 and 1965):

	Area, sq. mi.	Population, millions
Prewar Germany (1933)	181,738	65.9
Postwar Germany (united)	137,928	75.1
West Germany (1964)	96,114	58.0
East Germany (1963)	41,814	17.2
Great Britain (1963)	94,220	53.7
France (1963)	211,207	48.1
Italy (1963)	116,303	50.6

III. THE COMMON MARKET'S FEDERALIST EUROPE

1. There are, of course, three European Communities: the European Coal and Steel Community (1950), the European Economic Community, and the European Atomic Energy Community (1958). The present trend is towards uniting them into one body. Each shares the same membership and the same parliament, and by a decision of the Six in the spring of 1965, subject to the ratification of the national parliaments, the executives of all three are to be fused into a single body on January 1, 1966. This study has concentrated almost entirely on the activities of the Common Market as it is by far the most significant of the supranational bodies.

2. Walter Hallstein, *True Problems of European Integration*, p. 10.

3. For an excellent history of the European movement, see Brugmans, *L'Idée Européenne, 1918–1965.*

4. At the transition to the Third Stage, January 1, 1966. For a more detailed discussion, see Note 19, below.

5. The bureaucracy is called supranational because, though appointed to the Communities by the national governments, it neither receives orders from nor is responsible to the states, but rather acts "in the Community interest." Thus a new element is introduced which is independent of direct control by the states and has its own powers of initiative.

6. Kennedy's famous Atlantic Partnership speech on July 4, 1962 called for a Western alliance "built on two mighty pillars: America on the one side and an integrated Europe on the other." Hallstein, opposing Atlantic integration, responded enthusiastically. See Hallstein, *Partnership in the Making,* and *United Europe—Challenge and Opportunity,* p. 56. See Note 74.

7. See Anthony Nutting, *Europe Will Not Wait* (London, 1960), and J. H. Huizinga, *Confessions of a European in England* (London, 1958). There is also Lord Boothby's extraordinary speech in the House of Lords on June 30, 1960.

8. The Treaty of Dunkirk, signed between the French and English on March 5, 1947, technically established an alliance in case of future German aggression. Many saw it as the beginning of a full Anglo-French partnership to create a united Europe. While some institutions did follow, the hoped for result never materialized. See Brugmans, *L'Idée,* pp. 96–98.

9. For an account of these events, see "Origines et Elaboration du 'Plan Schuman'" in *Cahiers de Bruges* (Bruges, College d'Europe, 1953), No. IV.

10. Brugmans, *L'Idée,* p. 133.

11. Churchill remarked in 1953, "We are with them, not of them." Brugmans, *L'Idée*, p. 153. He saw "four pillars of the temple of peace"—a united Europe, the Soviet Union, the United States, and, significantly, the British Commonwealth. Eden got much of the blame for England's anti-European attitude. See Sir David Maxwell-Fyfe, *Political Adventure: The Memoirs of the Earl of Kilmuir* (London, Weidenfeld, 1964).

12. The plan for the European federal government was the work of the Common Assembly. A commission of specialists was set up under Heinrich von Brentano. See *Projet de Traité portant Statut de la Communauté Européenne*, Informations et Documents officiels de la Commission Constitutionnelle, Paris, Secrétariat de la Commission Constitutionnelle, mars-avril, 1953. Other plans submitted independently were: *Projet de Statut de la Communauté Politique Européenne*, le Mouvement Européen, Bruxelles, Editions du Comité d'Etudes pour la Constitution-européenne, 1952; Robert R. Bowie and Carl J. Friedrich, *Etudes sur le Fédéralisme*, Bruxelles, Mouvement Européen, 1952–1953.

13. Spaak told the Assembly at this time that there were not more than 60 members (out of 135) who believed in the need to create Europe. Brugmans, *L'Idée*, p. 123.

14. See Raymond Aron and Daniel Lerner, *France Defeats E.D.C.* (New York, Praeger, 1957).

15. Hallstein: "When we had first harmonized our policy on heavy industry, we thought the time had come for a common defense policy and even for a 'Political Community.' Disappointed in this, we returned to economic policy, this time with a success that surpassed all expectations." *Unity of the Drive for Europe*, p. 24.

16. It was at Messina, from June 1–3, 1955, that the six partners in the Coal and Steel Community decided to create the Common Market and Euratom. The Treaty of Rome was signed on March 26, 1957, and went into effect on January 1, 1958.

17. European Parliamentary Assembly, *Débats I*, January 13, 1959, pp. 223–280.

18. A recent book whose careful conclusions and voluminous studies have been much relied upon in my own study is Leon N. Lindberg, *The Political Dynamics of European Economic Integration*. See also, Ernst B. Haas, *The Uniting of Europe: Political, Social, and Economic Forces, 1950–1957*, and U. W. Kitzinger, *The Politics and Economics of European Integration*.

19. Decision making under the Treaty of Rome is extremely complicated. In some cases, the Council acts alone, in others, the Commission. In general, though, decisions are reached by the Council acting on a proposal of the Commission. The Treaty usually specifies the voting arrangements for each

type of decision. In the early stages, decisions usually required unanimity. After the Third Stage especially, decisions will, more often than not, require a qualified majority. Votes are weighted: France, Germany, and Italy each have four, Holland and Belgium, two, and Luxembourg, one. A majority of twelve votes out of seventeen is required. When the Council acts on a proposal coming from the Commission, the majority of twelve votes may be reached by the three big states alone; when the Council acts on its own, the majority of twelve must include at least four states. These provisions are meant to protect the small states from the large, it being presumed that the Commission is a special guardian of the small states. For a detailed analysis of this process, see Lindberg, Chap. III, and his App. A.

20. *Ibid.*, pp. 67, 68.

21. *Ibid.*, p. 294.

22. *Ibid.*, p. 284.

23. *Ibid.*, p. 286.

24. To cite a few examples: France was the Commission's closest ally in opposing the establishment of a Free Trade Area; France has consistently sent some of its ablest civil servants to Brussels; France proposed acceleration of the Treaty of Rome in 1959; French pressure will perhaps force the most difficult and significant step in economic integration, a common market in agriculture.

25. A point made frequently by students of the E.E.C. See Lindberg, pp. 288 ff.

26. Hallstein's view is not that the Common Market will pass from economic to political decisions, but that the so-called economic decisions are already highly political. Economics and politics are inextricably mixed because of "the increasing rôle played by Government in determining the conditions within which such economic activity takes place." Hallstein, *United Europe—Challenge and Opportunity*, p. 43.

27. *True*, p. 22.

28. *Faux*, p. 15.

29. Lindberg, p. 6. Lindberg includes the shifting of expectations and activities as part of his definition. The whole of his first chapter deals with the points referred to in Notes 29–32.

30. *Ibid.*, p. 9.

31. See Robert C. North, Howard E. Koch, Jr., and Dina A. Zinnes, "The Integrative Functions of Conflict," *Journal of Conflict Resolution*, IV (1960), 355–374.

32. See Ernst B. Haas, "International Integration: the European and the Universal Process," *International Organization*, XV (1961), 366–392.

33. Hallstein, *True*, pp. 25–29.

34. The disadvantages of not having a common spokesman and a common policy became apparent at the time of the negotiations with Britain over entry into the Common Market.

35. Efforts to develop community-wide planning are under way in Brussels, but have naturally met with tremendous difficulties, to begin with, because administrative practices vary so widely from country to country. Still, some significant progress has been made towards uniform statistics, methods of taxation, and welfare programs.

36. Lindberg, p. 291.

37. Trade growth among the Six (in millions of $):
     Total Imports, 1957: $7,032; 1963: $15,706.
     Total Exports, 1957: $7,154; 1963: $15,925.
Statistiques de Base de la Communauté, Office Statistique des Communautés Européenes, Bruxelles, 1964, Tableaux 67, 69.

38. See The Rt. Hon. Hugh Gaitskell, M.P. and the Rt. Hon. George Brown, M.P., *Britain and the Common Market*, text of speeches made at the 1962 Labour Party Conference with accepted policy statement (Labour Party Publication, London).

39. The E.E.C. has already shown an enormous increase in its general world trade (in millions of $):
     Total Imports, 1957: $24,816; 1963: $40,350.
     Total Exports, 1957: $22,440; 1963: $37,545.
Statistiques de Base, 1964, Tableaux 64, 65. (See Note 37.)

40. Lindberg, pp. 121, 172–3.

41. Hallstein, *True*, p. 17.

42. See, for example, the article by Raymond Aron, "Succès et Echec du Marché commun," *Le Figaro*, March 9, 1965, p. 1; or by Maurice Duverger, "Domination ou Voie Nouvelle," or by René Mayer, "Hegemonie ou Solidarité," *Le Monde*, November 21, 1964, p. 3.

43. Hallstein, *True*, pp. 26 ff.

44. The Commission took the occasion of the agricultural agreements to propose that all customs duties gradually revert to the Community, on industrial products as well as on agricultural products. In effect, each country would contribute to the Community income according to the volume of its extra-Community trade. Commission estimates placed France's share at 18 per cent of the Community's income, Germany's at 39 per cent, and thus, doubtless, hoped to tempt the French. Furthermore, the Commission

wanted the powers of the European Parliament over the budget greatly increased. See Notes 65 and 66. In the summer of 1965, France's rejection of the whole proposal precipitated a grave crisis in which France has threatened to withdraw from the E.E.C.

45. This is Lindberg's conclusion. This section was written before the crisis over agriculture during the summer, 1965. As this book goes to press, events would seem to confirm my conclusion stated here—that the major power resides with the national states, and that the dynamics of economic integration can be halted by a major state even without its withdrawing from the Community.

46. The French expect to develop both a more effective professional army and a nuclear deterrent for less money than they formerly spent on a large conscript army. Since 1953, defense expenditures have been cut from 11.0 per cent of the G.N.P. to 8.1 per cent in 1958 and to 6.4 per cent in 1963. Present estimates for defense are $29–30 billion from 1965–70. Annual defense expenditures are thus meant to be kept below 5 per cent of the G.N.P. Even this requirement allows some leeway. In a genuinely expanding economy, that 5 per cent becomes a larger sum each year. Furthermore, if other government expenditures are increased less than the growth in the G.N.P., even more money becomes available for military expenditures without either raising taxes or cutting nonmilitary expenditures. See the report on defense expenditures published annually by the Institute for Strategic Studies, London. See also, the account of the Assembly debate, *Le Figaro,* December 2, 1964, p. 6. The ability of the French to develop an effective deterrent is, of course, bitterly disputed. An excellent summary of the arguments against the French deterrent is "Force Nationale Stratégique, Défense et Politique Etrangère," *Bulletin intérieur de l'Association Socialisme et Democratie,* January, 1965. Any reckoning of the cost and benefits must include the effects on general technological development. I make no pretence to expert knowledge, but my conclusion is that the French can afford a nuclear force adequate for their strategic needs.

47. An empty-chair policy would not mean abrogating the Treaty of Rome or renouncing those decisions which had been made before. Yet without a state's participation, it would be impossible to continue to develop the Community, and would place the European movement in a sustained state of limbo.

48. Lindberg, pp. 84–85.

49. Sensible observers, when pressed, admit that the inexorable logic of economic integration, to have practical effect, requires the political support of the states. See Hallstein, *United Europe,* p. 38.

50. Hallstein, *True,* p. 3.

51. *Ibid.,* p. 1.

52. Federalist ideas were not unknown among the writers in the French Resistance. See Note 20, Chap. 1. Michel points out that Debré himself had a project for an Atlantic Community. See Michel, pp. 423–424.

53. De Gaulle, Press Conference, Algiers, April 21, 1944, in *Unity, Documents*, p. 327.

54. Hallstein, *Unity of the Drive*, p. 8.

55. *True*, p. 10.

56. *True*, p. 8; *Faux*, p. 4.

57. *True*, pp. 12 ff.

58. *Unity of the Drive*, p. 15.

59. *True*, p. 11.

60. *Ibid.*, p. 8.

61. *Faux*, p. 4.

62. Hallstein chides social science for being slow to appreciate the significance of the process of European integration. *True*, pp. 32–33.

63. Federalism would, of course, resolve some issues—such as ethnic and cultural minorities and boundary disputes between states.

64. Lindberg, pp. 86 ff, 260.

65. The Commission proposes that the Parliament, by a majority, be able to amend the original budget passed by the Council. These amendments would go into effect automatically after one month unless amended again by the Council. If the Commission were to support the Parliament's amendments, it would take five states on the Council to change them, otherwise only four. The Commission argues that since the large sum from tariffs would be escaping from national parliamentary control, the European Parliament must be strengthened as a substitute. See *Financement de la Politique Agricole Commune—Ressources propres de la Communauté—Renforcement des pouvoirs du Parlement Européen* (Propositions de la Commission au Conseil), Bruxelles, March 31, 1965, COM(65) p. 150. See also Note 44.

66. Article 138 of the Treaty of Rome calls for direct elections to the Parliament. Once elections are direct, the Commission report envisages "un pouvoir budgétaire complet au Parlement européen," p. 12, and "la compétence pour l'institution de recettes propres de la Communauté qui reste actuellement entre les mains des Etats membres." p. 11. *Financement de la Politique Agricole Commune*. See Note 65.

67. See Michel Debré, *Projet de Pacte pour une Union d'Etats Européens*. Debré, in this sketch of the hypothetical organization of Europe, suggests the need for an "arbitre," elected by universal suffrage, to head his European confederation. See also Note 52.

68. See Emile Benoit, *Europe at Sixes and Sevens* (New York, 1961), p. 14.

69. These views on other people's opinions are based upon extensive interviews with officials, partisans, and critics of the European Communities.

70. Hallstein, *True*, p. 32.

71. I owe this insight to a conversation with Altiero Spinelli.

72. See Bertrand de Jouvenel, "Du Principat."

73. Hallstein, *Unity of the Drive*, p. 6.

74. *Faux*, p. 23. See also Note 6.

IV. DE GAULLE'S NATIONALIST EUROPE

1. There are, of course, many distinguished Gaullists with important ideas of their own—Michel Debré, for example.

2. As an officer detailed to the Secrétariat Général de la Défense Nationale, de Gaulle studied carefully the plans that were being proposed by Tardieu and Paul-Boncour for an international police force. De Gaulle favored such international schemes as consistent with France's interest in preserving the *status quo*. An international police force, he argued, would have to be made up of highly mobile professional troops, the kind of army he was desperately urging France to build. *Vers l'armée*, pp. 95 ff.

3. As Reynaud's representative to Churchill in the last days of the Third Republic, de Gaulle was an important figure in the British offer to merge with the French government. See II, Note 20.

4. Speech, London, June 18, 1942 in *Discours*, Vol. I, p. 253.

5. *Unity, Documents*, p. 327.

6. Speech, Algiers, March 18, 1944 in *Unity, Documents*, pp. 259–260.

7. *Salvation*, p. 235.

8. *Ibid.*, pp. 50–53.

9. *Ibid.*, p. 253.

10. Speech, Lille, June 29, 1947, microfilm.

11. Communiqué du Conseil de Direction du R.P.F. sur le Conseil de l'Europe, August 7, 1947, microfilm.

12. Speech, Bordeaux, September 25, 1949, and Press Conference, November 14, 1949, microfilm. Both mirror the ideas of the R.P.F. communiqué mentioned above.

13. *France sera*, p. 297.

14. *Ibid.*, p. 289.

15. Press Conference, February 25, 1953, microfilm.

16. Declaration before the Anglo-American Press Association, September 12, 1951, microfilm.

17. Press Conference, September 5, 1960 in *Major Addresses*, p. 93.

18. It is said, on the other hand, that among some of the most prominent functionalists, there was more enthusiasm in the beginning for Euratom than for the E.E.C. The former filled much better the formula of a supranational body performing a particular function.

19. Address, April 19, 1963 in *Major Addresses*, p. 225. Press Conference, July 29, 1963, *ibid.*, p. 234.

20. Declaration, September 12, 1951, microfilm. See Note 16.

21. Speech, Sainte-Mandé, November 4, 1951, microfilm.

22. Speech, Nancy, November 25, 1951, microfilm.

23. Press Conference, December 21, 1951, microfilm.

24. Press Conference, November 14, 1949, and interview with M. Bradford as representative of U.P. at Colombey-les-deux-Eglises, July 10, 1950, microfilm.

25. Press Conference, January 14, 1963 in *Major Addresses*, p. 214.

26. Press Conference, May 15, 1962, *ibid.*, pp. 176–177.

27. Press Conference, January 14, 1963, *ibid.*, p. 213.

28. *Ibid.*, pp. 213–214.

29. A repeated exhortation, until recently. See Press Conference, February 25, 1953, microfilm. Compare with IV, Note 136.

30. Press Conference, September 5, 1960 in *Major Addresses*, pp. 92–93.

31. The plan was named after Christian Fouchet, currently the Minister of Education, who was France's representative at the negotiations. A collection of relevant documents and summary of events is found in Parlement Européen, *Le Dossier de l'Union Politique* (January, 1964).

32. The Germans are said to have objected because their Constitution, remembering Hitler, forbade the referendum. See Roger Massip, *De Gaulle et l'Europe*, p. 70.

33. *Ibid.*, p. 8.

34. See Paul-Henri Spaak, "New Effort to Build Europe." The Italians and Germans hoped for a meeting to discuss political unity in Venice during the spring, 1965, but the French refused, arguing that the time was not ripe.

35. The Franco-German Treaty calls for regular meetings of heads of state and ministers, and cooperation on a variety of levels of interest between the two nations. For the text, see *Le Dossier de l'Union Politique*. (See Note 31).

36. De Gaulle's family were upright, rather Jansenist Catholics, intensely patriotic, highly cultivated, and with monarchical and aristocratic sympathies. His father, Henri de Gaulle, taught and directed a number of academies for children from similar families. He was known as an excellent teacher of history and a man of admirable cultivation and character. De Gaulle's mother, born Josephine Maillot, was from the prosperous and dignified industrial bourgeoisie of the North. Her piety, according to her son, was equalled only by her patriotism. Both parents were much saddened by the social and political conflicts of the time which, they believed, gravely weakened the nation. Henri de Gaulle could not support the condemnation of the innocent Dreyfus, but deplored the antimilitary and anticlerical intentions of the Dreyfusards. See de La Gorce, Lacouture, Tournoux, or any of several other studies that deal with de Gaulle's early life.

37. The French titles are: *La Discorde chez l'ennemi; Le Fil de l'épée; Vers l'armée de métier; La France et son armée.* See the bibliography.

38. *Edge*, p. 9.

39. *Ibid.*

40. *Ibid.*, p. 10.

41. *La France et son Armée*, p. 1.

42. As de Gaulle saw it, the intrigues of generals and politicians, and the Kaiser's lack of firmness in supporting the Chancellor, Bethmann-Hollweg, led to several crucial mistakes in the conduct of the war and finally to Beth-

mann's fall. Thus in the moment of gravest crisis, when the military situation had worsened, there was only "un gouvernement sans indépendence et sans crédit. . . ." *Discorde,* p. 213. Germans called for a Clemenceau, *ibid.,* pp. 253–254.

43. The first three chapters, "The Conduct of War," "Of Character," and "Of Prestige," were new versions of the lectures. Chapter Four, "Of Doctrine," comes from an article written in 1925. De Gaulle added "Of Politics and the Soldier," and the Preface. See de La Gorce, pp. 66–67.

44. Pétain arranged for and attended the lectures. For a description, see Tournoux, Chap. VII.

45. *Edge,* p. 62.

46. *Ibid.,* p. 56.

47. *Ibid.,* p. 57.

48. "In the tumult of men and events, solitude was my temptation; now it is my friend." *Salvation,* p. 328.

49. *Edge,* p. 64.

50. *Ibid.,* p. 31.

51. *Ibid.,* pp. 63–64.

52. *Ibid.,* pp. 64–65.

53. *Ibid.,* p. 20.

54. Bergson in *ibid.,* p. 16.

55. *Ibid.,* p. 17.

56. *Ibid.,* pp. 24 ff. De Gaulle entered the French Army just before World War I in the midst of the doctrinal conflict between the advocates of offense at any price and those led by Pétain who emphasized defense and firepower. De Gaulle greatly admired Pétain in those days for his unshakable *mesure* and de Gaulle, in turn, became Pétain's valued protégé. In the 1930's, it would seem, de Gaulle's enthusiasm for mobile shock tactics drew him farther and farther away from his patron. A close study of their relations is Tournoux, *Pétain et de Gaulle.*

57. De Gaulle grew up in the midst of the great French intellectual revolt against scientific positivism, and that revolt naturally had great influence upon him. Bergson was its leading philosopher. The parallels between de Gaulle and Bergson are striking, although obviously there were many other influences on de Gaulle, and, no doubt, de Gaulle has many ideas to

which Bergson would not have subscribed. See, for example, Bergson's critique of nationalism in *The Two Sources of Morality and Religion*, 1932. Other leading figures in the movement included Boutroux, Péguy, Psichari, Barrès, Henri Massis, and Maurras. The milieu and its effect on de Gaulle is discussed in de La Gorce, Chap. 1. (See also Note 106.)

58. See *Edge*, pp. 51 ff. When asked in 1954 whether he would have tolerated, while he was in power, that a general officer or even a Marshall of France should refuse to obey his summons, de Gaulle replied: "I was France, the state, the government. I spoke in the name of France. I was the independence and the sovereignty of France. That is why, in the last analysis, everyone used to obey me." Press Conference, Paris, April 7, 1954, microfilm.

59. A relatively straightforward exposition of Nietzsche's ideas is his *Beyond Good and Evil*, 1886.

60. An exception might have occurred on June 20, 1929, a time of great personal and professional unhappiness for de Gaulle, when he wrote a now famous letter to his friend, Colonel Nachin, saying: "Ah! toute l'amertume qu'il y a de nos jours à porter le harnais! Il le faut pourtant. Dans quelques années, on s'accrochera à nos basques pour sauver la patrie . . . et la canaille par-dessus le marché. . . ." Lacouture, p. 31. There is a dispute as to whether de Gaulle wrote "nos" or "mes" basques. Tournoux, p. 134, notes that "canaille" can mean simply the common people without any implication of disdain, as in Victor Hugo: "La canaille suivait Jésus-Christ."

61. *Discorde*, p. x.

62. *La France et son Armée*, p. 109.

63. *Ibid.*, p. 150.

64. *Discorde*, p. x.

65. See, for example, *Vers l'Armée de Métier*, "Technique."

66. See *La France et son Armée*, "Grande Guerre."

67. *Vers l'Armée de Métier*, pp. 87–88.

68. *La France et son Armée*, p. 191.

69. *Ibid.*, p. 47.

70. See Lacouture, p. 184. The author opposes the baroque to the classic which is not my understanding of the term.

71. *Call,* Chap. 1 and 2.

72. At the end, Reynaud brought de Gaulle into his government as Under Secretary of State for National Defense, and sent him as his representative to Churchill to arrange the transfer of the government from Metropolitan France. See *Call,* Chaps. 1 and 2.

73. *Ibid.,* pp. 79–80.

74. *Salvation, Documents,* pp. 384–90.

75. De Gaulle's view of the Third Republic is captured in his description of an interview with Léon Blum. De Gaulle was pleading with the Premier for a policy that would strengthen France before it was too late: "During our conversation, the telephone had rung ten times, deflecting Léon Blum's attention to petty parliamentary or administrative questions. As I took my leave and he was again called, he made a great, tired gesture. 'Judge,' he said, 'if it is easy for the head of the government to hold to the plan you have outlined when he cannot remain five minutes with the same idea!' " *Call,* p. 26.

76. Throughout the *Memoirs* and his wartime speeches, de Gaulle rages against Vichy on the occasion of each of those sad conflicts between the Free French and those "well-intentioned Frenchmen" led astray by their mistaken sense of duty. It was the Germans and the Allies who benefited. See, for example, *Unity,* Chap. 1.

77. *Call,* p. 81.

78. *Unity,* p. 12.

79. *Salvation,* p. 169.

80. Press Conference, London, February 9, 1943. *Discours,* Vol. II, p. 26.

81. *Unity,* p. 293.

82. *Call,* p. 235.

83. *Ibid.,* p. 210.

84. See Milton Viorst, *Hostile Allies.*

85. *Unity,* p. 88.

86. *Ibid.,* p. 269.

87. *Ibid.*

88. *Ibid.,* p. 270.

89. *Ibid.,* p. 271.

90. *Ibid.*

91. See, for example, Press Conference, November 14, 1949, microfilm.

92. The First Appeal, London, June 18, 1940, *Discours*, Vol. I, p. 14.

93. French independence was the theme, for example, of the radio and television address of April 28, 1965.

94. Michel, *Les Courants de Pensée de la Résistance.*

95. *Salvation,* pp. 105–106.

96. *Salvation,* Chap. 3, "Order."

97. *Unity,* p. 172.

98. *Salvation, Documents,* p. 386.

99. *Ibid.,* p. 389.

100. *Ibid.,* p. 390.

101. *Ibid.,* p. 387.

102. *Ibid.*

103. Debré was censured over the *force de frappe* in December, 1961. Debré proposed new elections, but, in April, 1962, de Gaulle chose Pompidou as the new Premier. For a shrewd account of the complex issues, see de La Gorce, Chap. 17.

104. The official arguments for government control of radio and television and refusal to allow the opposition to use them, can be found in the various statements of the Minister of Information, Alain Peyrefitte, during the spring, 1965, session of the Assembly.

105. See *Memoirs,* e.g. *Unity,* 198.

106. Nicholas Wahl, "Aux Origines de la Nouvelle Constitution," *Revue Française de Science Politique,* March, 1959.

107. See II, Note 6.

108. See Bertrand de Jouvenel, "Du Principat."

109. It is argued by many students of French politics that de Gaulle's system will continue only if there develop strong parties capable of giving a government a firm majority. If any other President than de Gaulle challenged the Assembly in new elections or a referendum, he might lose, and effective government would be impossible. Therefore, the practical future of the Gaullist regime depends on developing the U.N.R. into a permanently strong party, only possible if the U.N.R. again wins a majority in the

1967 elections. The opposite thesis holds that any future president will be able to control Parliament now that the president is elected by direct suffrage. The people can be expected to act in a more rational fashion than the old Parliamentary government. The people, having chosen their chief, will continue to support him in referenda and Parliamentary elections. Even if the latter thesis should be valid, and de Gaulle seems to be leaning towards it, it is difficult to see how a new president can be nominated except through some institutionalized party mechanism. De Gaulle has given France its Washington; the U.N.R. may provide an Adams; but will there ever be a Jefferson?

110. While past votes indicate that de Gaulle is popular with the masses, a recent ACDA European Elite Survey suggests that he is also supported by a larger percentage of France's elite than one might suspect. For example, of a carefully chosen sample of 147 persons, a majority were moderately satisfied to highly satisfied with the present governmental system. A majority felt that there was some likelihood that the Fifth Republic would survive after de Gaulle, with a large percentage of this group quite sure it would. A majority believed that France would not return to the party system of the Fourth Republic. A majority saw an increasing tendency toward multipolarity in international politics and approved of the trend. Forty per cent felt that France had a "manifest destiny." I am grateful to the Yale Political Science Research Library for providing this information.

111. *Call,* p. 104.

112. *Salvation,* p. 86.

113. Speech on radio and television, April 27, 1965.

114. *Salvation,* p. 95.

115. The decision to build a French atomic force had been taken long before de Gaulle's return to power. By 1957, the Fourth Republic was said to have spent nearly $343 million on atomic research and development. By 1956, Guy Mollet, head of the Socialists and Premier at the time of the Suez crisis, was announcing that France would have the legal and material capacity to start military production by 1961. See Edgar S. Furniss, Jr., *France, Troubled Ally,* 264 ff.

116. Press Conference, January 14, 1963 in *Major Addresses,* pp. 216 ff.

117. *Ibid.,* p. 216.

118. *Ibid.,* p. 217.

119. *Salvation,* p. 58.

120. *Ibid.,* 59.

121. *Unity,* p. 253.

122. *Salvation,* p. 59.

123. *Ibid.,* 57.

124. See Note 121.

125. Press Conference, January 14, 1963 in *Major Addresses,* pp. 211 ff.

126. While de Gaulle has often sounded the alarm against external and internal communism, his fundamental attitude has been that communism will abate, but that Russia and France, linked by their fear of Germany, will remain. "In the ceaseless movement of the world, all doctrines, all schools, all rebellions, have only one time. Communism will pass. But France will not pass." *Call,* p. 269.

127. *Salvation,* p. 61.

128. The R.P.F., de Gaulle's postwar political movement, drew much of its strength from the fear of communism. See Lacouture, pp. 146 ff.

129. France: $857.9 million, 1.09 per cent of the G.N.P. The United States: $3.846 billion, 0.66 of 1 per cent of the G.N.P. Great Britain: $412.9 million, 0.50 of 1 per cent of the G.N.P. Portugal: $47.1 million, 1.65 per cent of the G.N.P. Joseph R. Slevin, *The New York Herald Tribune,* European Ed., November 5, p. 9.

130. Press Conference, January 31, 1964 in *Major Addresses,* p. 251.

131. Press Conference, May 15, 1962, *ibid.,* p. 175.

132. *Ibid.*

133. For probably the fullest exposition of the psychological basis of nationalism, see Bernard Bosanquet, *The Philosophical Theory of the State* (1910), and *The Psychology of the Moral Self* (1897).

134. See III, Note 67.

135. For a thorough and not discouraging analysis of the long-range possibilities for harmonization of the foreign policies of the European states, see Michel Massenet, "La Politique Extérieure d'une Europe Unie."

136. De Gaulle once wanted a federal French Union and Algerian integration, but concluded, first with Black Africa and then with Algeria, that nationalism was too strong and that a policy of national independence was all that was possible. After the war and in the R.P.F. days, de Gaulle used to speak optimistically, if cautiously, of the eventual possibility of a close and even a federal union in Europe. Since the failure of the Fouchet Plan, his public statements have grown more and more pessimistic. He observed at a recent garden party: "Les nations, ça existe. Il y a une Italie, une Allemagne. C'est millénaire, c'est bimillénaire." *Le Monde,* June 12,

1965, p. 2. For those who would blame the failure of Europe solely on de Gaulle, it is comforting to regard such remarks as statements of principle. It is quite possible they are the conclusions of a disillusioning experience.

V. AMERICA'S ATLANTIC EUROPE

1. See Leonard Beaton, "The Western Alliance and the McNamara Doctrine."

2. Several Frenchmen have expressed their disagreement with American strategic doctrine. Most sharply critical, perhaps, is Pierre Gallois. See his article, "Réflexions sur l'Evolution des Doctrines Américaines." For a criticism of Gallois's theories, see Kissinger, *Troubled Partnership*, p. 13. Other French strategists critical of American policy are Ailleret, Beaufre, and Billotte.

3. De Gaulle presented the essential argument at his press conference on January 14, 1963: ". . . the deterrent is now a fact for the Russians as for the Americans, which means that in the case of a general atomic war, there would inevitably be frightful and perhaps fatal destruction in both countries. In these conditions, no one in the world—particularly no one in America—can say if, where, when, how and to what extent the American nuclear weapons would be employed to defend Europe. Moreover, this does not in the least prevent the American nuclear weapons, which are the most powerful of all, from remaining the essential guarantee of world peace." *Major Addresses*, p. 217. The argument is essentially the same as de Gaulle had been urging since the founding of NATO. See his speech at Bordeaux, September 25, 1949, microfilm. For a fuller discussion of the complex strategic arguments, consult Kissinger, *Troubled Partnership*, Chap. 4, and Osgood, *Case for the MLF*.

4. Christian Herter quoted in Henry Kissinger, "Strains on the Alliance," *Foreign Affairs*, pp. 251–252.

5. "It is thus in relation to Europe that the paradox of increased reliance on conventional forces but no reduced reliance on nuclear weapons has come into focus." Morton H. Halperin, "The 'No Cities' Doctrine," *The New Republic*, p. 16. For a discussion of those elements in America's strategy which tend to confuse its allies, see Hans J. Morgenthau, "The Four Paradoxes of Nuclear Strategy," p. 23.

6. See Robert S. McNamara, Commencement Address, The University of Michigan, June 16, 1962.

7. See General Charles Ailleret, "Opinion sur la théorie stratégique de la 'flexible response.' "

8. General Lauris Norstad has long supported the view that Europe should have certain guarantees and a reasonable voice in the use of nuclear weapons: "As sovereign states, they feel that they need this to fulfill their duties to their own people as well as to the Alliance. These convictions are very real to the Europeans. I find them wholly reasonable. They must be accepted as a fact of life." Address, annual Printing Week Dinner, New York, January 17, 1963, "Authority over Nuclear Weapons," *Vital Speeches* (Feb. 15, 1963), p. 259. See also Henry A. Kissinger, "The Unsolved Problems of European Defense," and "Coalition Diplomacy in a Nuclear Age."

9. See, for example, Alastair Buchan, *NATO in the 1960's, passim.* Buchan calls for a reorganization of NATO.

10. See David Schoenbrun's seven articles on the private letters between de Gaulle, Eisenhower, and then Kennedy, in which de Gaulle insisted on an Alliance directorate of America, Britain, and France, and yet, in the American view, rejected any approach to positive study or discussion. "De Gaulle and the Anglo-Saxons." According to Kissinger, however, the United States, while rejecting the proposal because it believed it could not designate one European partner to speak for the others, made no effort to explore de Gaulle's views on a wider forum. Kissinger, *Troubled Partnership,* p. 55.

11. See Coral Bell, *The Debatable Alliance,* pp. 58 ff. For a discussion of the Macmahon Act and its effect on allied policy, see Leonard Beaton and John Maddox, *The Spread of Nuclear Weapons.*

12. Kissinger, *Troubled Partnership,* p. 226.

13. *Ibid.,* pp. 236 ff.

14. President Kennedy made his Atlantic Partnership speech in Philadelphia on July 4, 1962. The MLF had its origins in a proposal within the Eisenhower administration, December, 1960. The Kennedy administration suggested the idea again the following May, but not until the spring, 1962, did the Administration begin intensive study of the problem. The end of negotiations between Britain and the Common Market led the American government to pursue the plan, and by December, 1963, the Germans were in agreement and a number of other countries were considering the matter. See Osgood, *The Case for the MLF,* pp. 5–6.

15. See Hallstein, "Partnership in the Making."

16. See William Pfaff, "Our Outdated Vision."

17. This point is made most sharply in Ronald Steel, *The End of Alliance,* Chap. 5.

18. Walter Lippmann, *Western Unity and the Common Market,* p. 50.

19. *Ibid.,* p. 30.

20. *Ibid.,* pp. 8–9.

21. See de Gaulle, Press Conference, April 7, 1954, microfilm.

22. De Gaulle, Press Conference, July 29, 1963, "French-American Relations," *Major Addresses,* pp. 231–236.

23. See Kissinger, *Troubled Partnership;* Steel, *End of Alliance;* Liska, *Europe Ascendant.*

24. See Kissinger, *Troubled Partnership,* p. 244.

25. Irving Babbitt, *Democracy and Leadership* (Boston, 1924).

26. Arnold Toynbee, *America and the World Revolution* (London, 1962), p. 17.

27. See Michel Massenet, "La Politique Extérieure d'une Europe Unie." See IV, Note 135.

28. Kissinger, *Troubled Partnership,* pp. 235, 250.

VI. NOBODY'S EUROPE?

1. For a careful and imaginative discussion of the whole question of nuclear stalemate, see George Liska, *Europe Ascendant,* pp. 150 ff. I believe it was Liska who suggested to me in conversation the notion of the "phantom world."

2. See IV, Notes 109, 110.

3. That seems the belabored and belated conclusion of Paul-Henri Spaak. See IV, Note 34.

Bibliography

As the scope of this study has been large, the possible bibliography is enormous. There is, for example, a recent bibliography of over 200 pages of titles on European intergration, L. L. Paklons, *Bibliographie Européenne*, Bruges, 1964. I have referred to many works in the notes, but list here only those relatively few books and articles which were either in constant use as sources or particularly provocative in leading me to my own conclusions.

Ailleret, Charles, "Opinion sur la Théorie Stratégique de la 'Flexible Response,'" *Revue de Défense Nationale* (August–September, 1964), p. 1323.

Albrecht-Carrié, René, *One Europe: The Historical Background of European Unity*. Garden City: Doubleday, 1965.

Beaton, Leonard, "The Western Alliance and the McNamara Doctrine," *Adelphi Papers*, The Institute for Strategic Studies, No. 11. London, August, 1964.

Beaton, Leonard, and Maddox, John, *The Spread of Nuclear Weapons*. London and New York: Praeger, 1962.

Bell, Coral, *The Debatable Alliance: An Essay in Anglo-American Relations*. London: Oxford University Press, 1964.

Bowie, Robert R. and Friedrich, Carl J., *Etudes sur le Fédéralisme*, 2 vols. Bruxelles: Movement Européen, 1952–1953.

Brugmans, Henri, *L'Idée Européenne, 1918–1965*. Bruges, 1965.

———. *Panorama de la Pensée Fédéraliste*. Paris: La Colombe, 1956.

Buchan, Alastair, *NATO in the 1960's: The Implications of Interdependence*. London: Chatto and Winders, 1963.

Calleo, David P., *Coleridge and the Idea of the Modern State*. To be published by Yale University Press, 1966.

Debré, Michel, *Projet de Pacte pour une Union d'Etats Européens*. Paris: Nagel, 1950.

Deutsch, Karl W., *Nationalism and Social Communication*. Princeton, 1960.

Le Dossier de l'Union Politique, Recueil de Documents avec Préface de M. Emilio Battista, Parlement Européen, Commission Politique, Direction Générale de la Documentation Parlementaire et de l'information, January, 1964.

European Integration and Economic Reality, Semaines de Bruges, 1964. Bruges, 1964.

Financement de la Politique Agricole Commune—Ressources Propres de la Communauté—Renforcement des Pouvoirs du Parlement Européen (Propositions de la Commission au Conseil), COM(65) 150. Bruxelles, March 31, 1965.

Friedrich, Carl J., "New Tendencies in Federal Theory and Practice," General Report, Sixth World Congress, International Political Science Association, Geneva, September 21–25, 1964.

Furniss, Edgar S., Jr., *France, Troubled Ally: De Gaulle's Heritage and Prospects*. New York: Harper, 1960.

Gallois, Pierre M., "Réflexions sur l'Evolution des Doctrines Américaines," *Revue de Défense Nationale* (July, 1964), p. 1219.

de Gaulle, Charles, *La Discorde chez l'Ennemi*. Paris: Berger-Levrault, 1944.

————. *Discours*, 3 vols. (Juin, 1940–Septembre, 1945). Paris: Le Cri de la France, 1944–45.

————. *The Edge of the Sword*. New York, 1960.

————. *La France et Son Armée*. Paris: Plon, 1938.

————. *La France Sera la France*, Discours, 1947–1951, ed. Rassemblement du Peuple Français.

————. *Major Addresses, Statements and Press Conferences of General Charles de Gaulle*, May 19, 1958–January 31, 1964. New York: French Embassy, Press and Information Division, 1964.

————. Speeches, statements and press conferences, 1946–1958. R.P.F. files, on microfilm, Bibliothèque de Fondation Nationale des Sciences Politiques.

————. *Vers l'Armée de Métier*. Paris: Berger-Levrault, 1944.

————. *The War Memoirs of Charles de Gaulle:*

The Call to Honor, 1940–1942. New York: Simon & Schuster, 1958.

Unity, 1942–1944. New York: Simon & Schuster, 1959.

Unity, Documents. New York: Simon & Schuster, 1960.

Salvation, 1944–1946. New York: Simon & Schuster, 1960.

Salvation, Documents. New York: Simon & Schuster, 1960.

Granet, Marie, *Défense de la France: Histoire d'un Mouvement de Résistance* (1940–1944). Paris: Presses Universitaires de France, 1960.

Grosser, Alfred, *La Politique Extérieure de la Ve République*. Paris: Editions du Seuil, 1965.

Haas, Ernst B., "International Integration: the European and the Universal Process," *International Organization*, XV, 1961.

————. *The Uniting of Europe: Political, Social, and Economic Forces, 1950–1957*. Stanford, 1958.

Hallstein, Walter, "Constitutional Problems of the European Community," Address, Bologna, May 15, 1965 (6273/x/65-E).

————. "Partnership in the Making," Speech, The Economics Club of New York, April 24, 1962, in *Vital Speeches*, June 1, 1962, p. 492.

————. "Some of Our 'Faux Problèmes,'" Stevenson Memorial Lecture, Royal Institute of International Affairs, Chatham House, London, December 4, 1964 (13668/x/64).

————. "The True Problems of European Integration," Address, Kiel, February 19, 1965 (2373/x/65).

————. "United Europe—Challenge and Opportunity," Clayton Lecture, Fletcher School of Law and Diplomacy, April 16, 1962 (2738/PP/62-En).

————. "The Unity of the Drive for Europe," Address, Rome, October 15, 1964 (11274/x/64).

Halperin, Morton H., "The 'No Cities' Doctrine," *The New Republic*, October 8, 1962.

Hamon, Léo, and Mabileau, Albert, eds., *La Personnalisation du Pouvoir*. Paris: Presses Universitaires de France, 1964.

Jouvenel, Bertrand de, "Du Principat," Article, Sixth World Congress, International Political Science Association, Geneva, September 21–25, 1964.

Kissinger, Henry A., "Coalition Diplomacy in a Nuclear Age," *Foreign Affairs*, July, 1964.

————. "Strains on the Alliance," *Foreign Affairs*, January, 1965.

————. *The Troubled Partnership*, New York: McGraw-Hill, 1965.

————. "The Unsolved Problems of European Defense," *Foreign Affairs*, July, 1962.

Kitzinger, U. W., *The Politics and Economics of European Integration*. New York: Praeger, 1963.

Lacouture, Jean, *De Gaulle*. Paris: Editons du Seuil, 1965.

La Gorce, Paul-Marie de, *De Gaulle Entre Deux Mondes: Une Vie et une Epoque*. Paris: Fayard, 1964.

Lindberg, Leon N., *The Political Dynamics of European Economic Integration*. London: Oxford University Press, 1963.

Lippmann, Walter, *Western Unity and the Common Market*. London: H. Hamilton, 1962.

Liska, George, *Europe Ascendant: The International Politics of Unification*. Baltimore: Johns Hopkins, 1964.

Macmahon, Arthur W., *Federalism, Mature and Emergent*. New York: Doubleday, 1958.

Massenet, Michel, "La Politique Extérieure d'une Europe Unie," *Futuribles, Bulletin SEDEIS*, 1964.

Massip, Roger, *De Gaulle et l'Europe*. Paris: Flammarion, 1963.

McNamara, Robert S., Commencement Address, The University of Michigan, June 16, 1962, in *Vital Speeches*, "The United States and Western Europe," August 1, 1962, p. 626.

Michel, Henri, *Les Courants de Pensée de la Résistance*. Paris: Presses Universitaires, 1961.

Morgenthau, Hans J., "The Four Paradoxes of Nuclear Strategy." *The American Political Science Review*, March, 1964.

Nathan, Roger, *Vers l'Europe des Réalités*. Paris: Plon, 1963.

Osgood, Robert E., *The Case for the MLF: A Critical Evaluation*. The Washington Center of Foreign Policy Research, 1964.

Parodi, Jean-Luc, *Les Rapports entre le Legislatif et l'Executif sous la Ve Republique*, Paris: Fondation Nationale des Sciences Politiques, 1962.

Passeron, André, *De Gaulle Parle*. Paris: Plon, 1962.

Pffaf, William, "Our Outdated Vision," *The Commonweal*, December 18, 1964, p. 411.

Schoenbrun, David, "De Gaulle and the Anglo-Saxons," *Le Figaro*, July 9–17, 1964.

Spaak, Paul-Henri, "New Effort to Build Europe," *Foreign Affairs*, January, 1965, p. 199.

Steel, Ronald, *The End of Alliance: America and the Future of Europe.* New York, 1964.

Tournoux, J-R., *Pétain et de Gaulle.* Paris: Plon, 1964.

Viorst, Milton, *Hostile Allies: FDR and de Gaulle.* New York: Macmillan, 1965.

Voyenne, Bernard, *Histoire de l'Idée Européenne.* Paris: Payot, 1964.

Wahl, Nicholas, "Aux Origines de la Nouvelle Constitution," *Revue Française de Science Politique,* March, 1959.

Wilcox, Francis O., and Haviland, H. Field, Jr., eds., "The Atlantic Community: Progress and Prospects," *International Organization,* Vol. XVII, No. 3, Summer, 1963.

Wiliams, Philip, *Crisis and Compromise.* New York: Oxford University Press, 1964.